AMBITION

—— ALPHA A. TIMBO ——

The Inside Secrets

as We Journey Towards

Our **GOD** *Given* **PURPOSE**.

 FriesenPress

Suite 300 - 990 Fort St
Victoria, BC, V8V 3K2
Canada

www.friesenpress.com

ISBN
978-1-5255-2407-3 (Hardcover)
978-1-5255-2408-0 (Paperback)
978-1-5255-2409-7 (eBook)

1. SELF-HELP, MOTIVATIONAL & INSPIRATIONAL

Distributed to the trade by The Ingram Book Company

*

First and foremost, I would like to thank my Lord and my God Jesus Christ for giving me the inspiration and will to write this amazing book. This book was written in response to the depths of some of the most difficult experiences and challenges I've had to endure in my life. The wisdom, knowledge, and gifts I attained during that season and process allowed me to be able to write a book of such value, full of insights and a definite eye-opener for the reader to discover themselves and what they are destined to become.

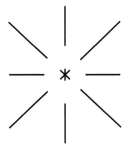

Table of Contents

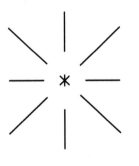

INTRODUCTION

When you look around and see all that God created in nature and all around the earth, from the skies to the trees and even the oceans and its inhabitants, it is clear that all have a purpose. The stars that brighten the second heaven, and the moon that reflects the light from the amazing sun, shining through the night at parts of the rotating Earth where the sunlight cannot reach, all have a purpose. The clouds that give rain, and the air that directs it to its designated location, have a purpose. The trees that were never planted by human hands, the magnificent mountains that stand tall above all others, the flowers that bloom in their season—everything on this Earth has a purpose. As we look at nature and gaze at all creation, we see that it is beautiful, carefully thought-out, and well-built. And of all God's creations, the most magnificent and unique is humanity. You.

Every human consists of three parts, three entities combined to make one: the spirit, the soul, and the body. The "body" gives us the practical ability to function here on Earth. The "spirit" consists of all you are: your identity, from your gifts and talents to the supernatural information embedded within you to bless the Earth and all its inhabitants. And then there is the soul, which is the mediator of the two, transferring all the information, gifts, and talents from the spirit to the body, allowing the supernatural to manifest in the natural realm, through you, and hence fulfilling your purpose on earth.

In many cases, we've being deceived by our communities, neighborhoods, friends, and even our families, to believe that we *are* whatever we are born into. Not so. If your original situation is a mess or dysfunctional, you were not born into it to *be* it. You were born into it to *change* it. Your purpose lies beneath the things around you, with those things that you deeply want to change, and the difference you want to make in your life and in the lives of others. There are many gifts within you, as well as all the resources you need to help you fulfill your purpose. Although your internal purpose is crying out loud to you, the noise and cares of this life can make your ears deaf to it.

Have you ever felt like there is something more to life? Have you ever felt as though you are more than what your situation is telling you? Have you ever felt like there is more to you than what people see? Have you ever felt like there is something greater in you, but that you do not know what it is?

That is PURPOSE, and it's calling out to you. Purpose is very much alive within you and it uses different methods to get you to discover it. In this book, I will talk about one of those methods—the driving force that pushes you to recognize it in a world that's full of distractions, detours, and turmoil.

It is called AMBITION: an eager or strong desire to become something.

As I always say, ***"Ambition is purpose in its baby stages; if guided and patiently worked on, it can be the engine for anyone to be all that they could be, living a life of PURPOSE."*** I believe this book is going to help you do just that!

CHAPTER 1
WHAT IS AMBITION?

Ambition is an eager or strong desire to achieve something, such as fame or power—the object or goal desired. I like the term "fame or power," for what most humans do not realize is that fame and power are already embedded within us. They're not something we need to seek, or even *should* seek. For in seeking them, we tend to fall into the countless dangers that this sinful world has placed in our way to take us off our course. Many people have scorned the idea of ambition and what it represents—and rightfully so, because many have taken that which is supposed to drive us toward something good and used it instead to seek fame and fortune, to gain power and influence in order to fulfill their own carnal agendas, to benefit themselves instead of others. Time and again, we see the damage that powerful people cause to themselves, their communities, and even their countries, constantly making selfish decisions inspired by misguided, misdirected ambition.

Ambition is not the problem. The problem lies in the nature or character of the individuals who use that good thing within them solely to achieve their carnal goals: gun violence, prostitution, corruption in government and business, deception, adultery, and more. It is disturbingly easy to illustrate the danger and prevalence of completely misdirected ambition.

Ambition with carnality

Note: Ambition misunderstood or misguided can lead one onto a path that will eventually cause self-destruction.

I have watched many people direct their ambition to the wrong things, like cars, houses, a celebrity status, the opposite sex, and (most common of all) the accumulation of money. Most of these people fall on their journey. And as for the minority who make it, they often do so at the expense of losing their integrity and the good character that people once knew them to possess. This world is encumbered with wants and needs that one *has* to meet, and often on a daily basis. Our bills, debts, clothes, kids, and transportation are just a few things that motivate us to wake up every morning in order to sustain ourselves and our loved ones. Sometimes, people realize that they have had enough, and allow their ambition to drive them to become more than what they currently are, according to their situations. If they're not careful, this desire for change can be stirred by misguided motives and evil agendas.

The drive to become much more than they are is not wrong, but the motives and agendas can be. We all want to drive nice cars, live in beautiful homes, and be financially free. We want to be able to have the resources to do what we want, to go where we want to go, and to buy what we want to buy. From the latest gadgets to fine clothing and shoes, we want to have it all. Having all the comforts that life has to offer is every-one's dream . . . in a world that's well known to shatter dreams. Having financial success, with all its inherent amenities, is great, but that ought not to be what drives us. When one who's driven in the right direction by their ambition begins to walk in their *purpose*, all those other things will automatically follow.

I know a story of a wise storekeeper who loved his customers and knew what their desired product was the moment they walked into his store. One day, a regular customer came in and asked for a bunch of tools to fix his old wooden table. When the man had gathered all the tools he desired, the total price was over $500. The man was frustrated that he was not able to afford them. The storekeeper, seeing the frustration on the face of one of his favorite customers, said, "Why don't you buy this beautiful wooden table from me, for $50? Whatever is in its drawer is yours. Then, maybe, if you come back in a few days, the prices of these tools will have gone down, based on the market."

The man agreed, and bought the wooden table from his good friend the storekeeper, for $50. As heavy as the table was, the man didn't hesitate to use all his strength to lift it up and put it in his truck. He arrived home with anticipation, and couldn't wait to open the wooden table's drawer to see what was inside. He used the key the storekeeper had given him to open the wooden drawer and, to his surprise, he saw all the tools that he had originally desired, in better colors and condition than the ones he wanted to purchase. There were even a few extra things in there that he would never have been able to afford. Now, he had a new table and all the tools he would ever want to fulfill the task ahead of him.

Why did I tell this story? When we allow our ambition to focus on purpose, all the materialistic things we wanted will automatically come with the package, without chasing or pushing for them. Most times, we do not know what lies inside the "wooden drawer" of our God-given purposes.

Note: Ambition fed by the "lust of the eyes" is sure to bring one to an unfortunate demise!

Ambition with immorality

I mentioned earlier about people allowing their ambition to lead them to do immoral things, dishonoring themselves in order to get to their desired end. *"What does it profit any to gain the world and lose their soul?"* Mark 8:36. In the times in which we live, people will do just about anything to get to the top, from adultery to fornication, lying to cheating (whether in relationships or in business). Indeed, they'll do whatever it takes, even selling all that they hold dear—including themselves—to gain something that seems like the world to them, when real freedom begins with you and how you measure yourself, not with expecting someone else to give it to you. I've seen this lead to marriages broken, friendships shattered, and occupations destroyed, all due to someone deciding to sell themselves short, going down paths that seemed right at that moment, but were far from it. Immoral acts don't just destroy one's career or reputation, they contaminate your God-given purpose and eventually suck you into a dark world that's filled with dangerous pitfalls and horrendous uncertainties.

Note: What is man without integrity, and what is the meaning of success without character?

We live in a world that makes it seem OK to take part in all forms of immorality in order to "make something" of ourselves. The truth is that, though you look good and normal on the outside, you are full of insecurities, flaws, and low self-esteem on the inside. The list goes on, but you know that the things you took part in, behind closed doors, in order to get to where you wanted to be—things that have stripped from you your self-worth and value.

The journey from the birth stages of our ambition to the discovery of who we are and the purpose embedded in us is all a part of the process. Most people are focused solely on the end result, when in actual fact, they should be focused on the experiences and the journey that lead them there. For some, a few stumbling blocks and tests of their character scare them, so they, sadly, yield to temptation. There will always be an end result. So when you do get there, it's not where you are that you reminisce about, but what you did and had to go through in order to get there. It would be a pity if those memories were filled with immorality, and the realization that you cheated yourself and sold yourself out just so you could get where you wanted to be. Though you might take pleasure in all your achievements, when you close your doors and look in the mirror, you don't even see the glamorous life and persona that others see in you, because of what you've done.

Immorality driven by ambition will suffocate all that you are and are born to be. You will become someone else, and the evidence of your true identity will be locked away in the chambers of your soul. Despite the fame and fortune, you will always be empty, needy, and wanting more. You will never be fulfilled and never satisfied because you never allowed the fullness of your journey to bring forth the perfection in you.

Note: A person driven by "the lust of the flesh" is no more than an animal walking on two legs.

Ambition with pride

Pride was the first sin to manifest, and it's very much alive within us today. Governments have been dismantled by it, neighborhoods crushed by it, and marriages broken by it. Families are in conflict and separated, and friendships torn apart—all because of pride. In every avenue of life, we see that pride has some form of influence. Ambition driven by pride can cause one to feel an unduly high opinion of their own self-worth.

Someone once told me, *"A humble person can travel the whole world without a penny, and still survive, for their humility can cause people to have favor with them."*

I cannot say the same for people with pride, who tend to subconsciously push others away rather than pull them in. In most cases, they want to become all that they can be because they feel like they are better than everyone, and know more, as well.

Note: Ambition driven by pride is no different than a trailer truck going downhill with no brakes, waiting for something to crash into head-on.

There is no attribute I know that has the designation of "downfall" written all over it more than pride. The bible teaches that *"pride goes before destruction and a haughty spirit before a fall." Prov. 16: 18.* It is the essence of failure and the foundation of all negativity. Pride is sometimes seen in those who want to prove that they are more important and better than everyone else. The truth is that they are trying to hide their past downfalls, insecurities, and insufficiencies, so they seek to replace their shame with pride and some assurance of self-worth by showing people that they are more than the sum of their own personal failures—even though that is how they have come to perceive themselves.

Note: Pride will allow you to overlook the integrity and character of good people, because you feel intimidated by them.

Pride will allow you to open the doors of your secret treasures and invite all types of people inside, in order to get praise and accolades, all the while overlooking the fact that some of those visitors have come to rob you. It is a flaw that negates potential business partnerships and strips opportunities from you. It shuts down your creative potential and makes you settle for only that which you know—and if you are not where you want to be, then it's fair to say that you actually don't know much.

Pride has been the root of the downfall of many people, past and present, from kings and leaders to the lowliest citizen, and there is no doubt that it will continue to be so in the future. This world has, unfortunately, taught us that being humble will make some of us vulnerable, *but being humble doesn't mean that you are a pushover. It just means that you're slow to speak, eager to learn, quick to hear, and OK with starting from the bottom . . . but not to stay there.*

Ambition with integrity

*Note: **Ambition** combined with **integrity** is like a tree in the midst of water; it always has the source to make it bear fruit.*

We live in a world that has totally forgotten what it means to have integrity. Before the success, fame, and status, before the money and even before relationships, before leaving the boat of safety and taking a step into the ocean of the world, one must first attain integrity. *Integrity is not merely something you attain for others—though they will be blessed by it— but a gift you give to yourself.*

Even if all else fails, you owe it to yourself to be able to search within and find that you have maintained the character and personality upon which the good nature of your spirit was built. Like I said, ambition is not the problem, but rather the character of the individual carrying it.

All throughout my life, I've seen many achieve great things, from celebrities to politicians, ministers to bishops, regular employees to CEOs, and I've come to the conclusion that the happiest and most-fulfilled people are those who maintained their integrity throughout their journey. Though ambition is the driving force, integrity is the source that keeps you stable in the storms and helps maintain focus and identity— where you are coming from and where you are going. Most people make one of two mistakes: Either they never think about integrity at all or they become so focused on what they want that they sell themselves short in carnality, immorality, or pride, and so forget about the integrity with which they started.

Note: The cares of life have enough darkness in them to suffocate the good values with which one was brought up.

It is the right of all mankind to achieve something great, but those who do it with integrity are the ones whose legacy lives on forever. Integrity is an attribute that one owes to themselves, by being honest with themselves in all that they do, making them incorruptible in life. *For riches, fame, and status do not make you whole as a person but rather make you become more of what you already are.*

With that being said, if wickedness, immorality, and pride are already planted within you, when you become rich or successful, you have only achieved resources that will feed the evil that you've become. But if you then become successful with integrity, which in truth would be a more challenging journey, you will have access to resources that would help you create more of yourself and influence the communities, people, and even the nation of which you are a part of.

There have been many leaders who allowed their ambition and personal motives to be their driving force: Nelson Mandela, Hitler, Mother Teresa, Queen (Bloody) Mary, George Washington, and Kim Jong-il, just to name a few. All of these men and women, in their respective places, became leaders in their countries. They all allowed the resources they attained to help them be more of what they already were. I'll leave it to you to decide which ones did it with integrity, and which ones sold their souls for fortune and power.

The journey to becoming successful and the ambition that drives it, are not solely based on the end result but, rather, on what you learn, and the experiences you go through in the process of becoming what you are destined to be. That is the *key*. Do we all want to see the end result? Of course we do. But what is the meaning of the end result if you have missed what you have experienced or forgotten what you've learned along the way, and are unable to pass the wisdom to someone else? *In a nutshell, the end result will have no value if the tools and experiences that come along the way are ignored.* I believe that keeping your integrity in all that you do will help you to maintain all the goodies you accumulate from past experiences, which will live on even long after you're gone.

CHAPTER 2
WHAT IS PURPOSE?

Note: Purpose is the function of a particular thing or being, in a particular area or place, that their creator or inventor intended it or them to be.

The essence of what makes us who we are, and the nature of the characteristics with which we were born, is solely based on our "purpose," or what we are to become. A man—by which I mean human—does not know what he truly is until he has discovered the purpose for which he was called. Entering an extravagant garden, a flower can look beautiful on the outside, but if it doesn't release the awesome fragrance within it, it hasn't really tapped into its fullest potential. A small mustard seed cannot be judged by its appearance as a seed but, rather, by what it can become when planted: the largest tree in the garden. It is the same with us. Purpose is the beginning and end of everything. It is the reason for existence. The importance of knowing one's purpose is as vital as the air we breathe.

There is nothing that we see with our human eyes that doesn't have purpose, whether or not we created it. And the same is true of ourselves, including our characteristics, behaviors, personalities, gifts, etc. It all has a purpose. Without purpose, the earth would be empty.

Purpose in animal-kind Mammals, birds, amphibians, invertebrates . . . all of animal-kind discover their purpose in the form of instincts, received at the moment of birth or existence. Have you ever wondered how the lion cub knows that it needs to search for its mother's milk as soon as it is born? They do it by instinct. The calf of a wildebeest learns to walk about five minutes after it's born; instinctively, it knows it has to learn this skill or it will fall prey to predators. Animals know, without being taught, that they have to hunt and kill, protect and nurture. They know that they must survive, and carry on their genes to ensure the survival of their species. Instincts embedded within them help them to adjust to and survive the particular environment in which they are placed, taking part in a circle of life that makes them who they are. Their function or *purpose* is understood or discovered based on their instincts.

Purpose of trees and their kind

Trees or plants, whether planted by mankind or not, do not move from one place to another. We can easily conclude that their purpose is effective and/or useful within the environment where they take root. Most of us know that we depend on the oxygen that trees produce to breathe. Do we also know that trees and plants provide the shade and shelter for animals like squirrels, birds, and even creeping things? They provide thousands of amazing fruits in all shapes, sizes, and flavors, all across the world, which we can either eat or use to produce drinks. Naturally, trees or plants receive and absorb moisture through their roots, and with the help of the sun, produce their fruits in their season, joining their circle of life and fulfilling their purposes in their particular environments.

Purpose in mankind

For mankind, it is much different. Though our purpose is embedded in us, rather than acting on it in response to instincts, we grow to discover and understand it. Good parents are not defined solely based on whether they feed or clothe their children. Their most important role is observing their children's personalities and characteristics in their toddler stages, which helps to reveal their gifts and talents. Though not knowing their offspring's full purpose, good parents can help put them in programs or environments that can stir or reveal the greatness in them at a very early age.

Humans, in most cases, can be easily deceived or misguided based on what we are introduced to at a very early age. As we become adults, we tend to become like those who surround us, whether they are good or bad. The reason the world is in the state it's in today, from murders, rape, abuse, terrorism, corruption, gang violence, and much more, is because the purpose of its general populations wasn't realized early, and something else filled in to try to replace their original reasons for existence. When not noticed at an early age, whatever replaces it can be very destructive to the individual and those around them. Purpose can also be buried under the influence of the communities into which we are born— neighborhoods, and the systems or traditions of a particular group of people or environment—and it can even be buried when surrounded by people of mediocrity.

These examples can be a curse for the purpose within an individual, and in most cases, it helps dig a grave within them in which they bury their greatness and the reason for their existence. There is an old saying: *"It takes a whole village to raise a child."* The problem is that, in the world in which we are living today, the villages, communities, cities, and nations have succumbed to war, gang violence, conflicts, and/or man-made traditions in certain groups. Sadly, our children and youths live mostly within these circumstances. They are misguided and deceived into thinking that is what they are.

The good news is that, unless they have truly been consumed by what they are introduced to, the purpose within will constantly nudge the individual, reminding them that they can become something more. Some of the nudgings can easily be missed, but depending on the individual, others can be very evident. *The discomfort,* and, sometimes, *lack of fulfillment,* we feel in a particular environment can be signs that you do not belong there.

It is your purpose within, letting you know that it's being suffocated.

Sometimes our surroundings can either make us or destroy us. Our purpose, when discovered early, can help us challenge or fight against that which is wrong around us. Though the habits and ways of life in that particular environment might be uncommon and unfruitful to the individual who knows their purpose, that same environment would seem common or the norm to those around them. Though they are the ones who are strange, they would think you are strange for not feeling as at home there as they do—because their blinded eyes can only understand what they have been introduced to.

It is not their fault; it is just that they have never left or seen what's outside of the box. Distractions, whether from friends, family, or even the cares of life, can accumulate and grow into stronger detours, steering us away from our purpose. These also sometimes rob us of the opportunity to discover our God-given purpose.

People who have discovered their purpose sometimes get upset and weary with the family and environment into which they were born, and start making excuses for why they are not where they are supposed to be in life. But even though people are sometimes born into bad communities, families, countries, and even traditions and systems, no one said they are supposed to blend into them. They are supposed to change it. Purpose is the reason, meaning, and essence of all life, and without it, one is merely wasted space, waiting to be replaced by another.

Not knowing your purpose can easily lead you to fall into many pitfalls—some so deep that it can take a lifetime to get out—leading to dysfunctional behaviors. There is a saying, that goes, *"If you don't stand for something, you'll fall for anything."* In bad communities or neighborhoods, young people try to fit in with gangs in order to fill the emptiness within them. In high school, they look for a crowd to associate themselves with, and if that crowd partakes in drugs, then they will partake in them, as well, just to fit in. Since they don't know their identity, or purpose, they go out looking for one, and accept whatever they are surrounded by or introduced to. For thugs, it's gangs. For addicts, it's drugs. For some, it's sex or relationships, which can lead to prostitution or sex trafficking or even broken hearts. For some, religion can keep an individual from discovering their purpose or true potential, based on the traditions, systems, and man-made rules that they have been brought up with. Though not fruitful for them, they believe it to be a good thing, because everyone around them is saying and doing the same thing and are OK with it. Another dysfunction in opposition to the discovery of purpose is thinking of yourself more highly than you should. It is not wrong to want to become great or do great things. The problem comes when your actions and motives are motivated by how great you want to become and to get the benefits that come with it.

Note: The greatest motive or achievement in life is realizing that whatever you become, great or small, should give you the ability to impact, change, or inspire the life of another.

In some cases, though we have discovered our purpose (even if we have yet to attain it), we want to become it or have it for the wrong reasons, or so that we can assure ourselves that we are something. Sometimes, even though our purpose has been discovered, we have insecurities, low self-esteem, and shortcomings that, when not tended to, can make us hide behind pride, or take negative actions to prove our self-worth to those around us.

This can happen in any environment, good or bad, and can choke our purpose and suffocate the process of fulfilling it. By humbly searching for and discovering your purpose, you can be satisfied in knowing that your life has value and you have a major role to play on Earth. With this revelation, you can easily find confidence, wholeness, courage, awareness, and the right associations and surroundings, based on what you have discovered about yourself. By discovering your purpose and the reason for your life, even if you are not there yet, you have the advantage of being able to make the right decisions and surround yourself with people who can help catapult you to your destiny.

CHAPTER 3
BASIC AMBITION

The term ambition has been so misused that most people, especially in an environment of mediocrity, presume it to be an evil thing. Now, of course, this doesn't apply to those who are in mediocrity and see themselves becoming more than what their current state is telling them, or even those who are just fine with where they are and are simply minding their own business, living their lives and not even looking at anyone else's. But what some folks do not realize is that we, as human beings, subconsciously act upon some form of ambition on a daily basis, and just do not realize it. As a matter of fact, we do it so much that it has become the norm for us in our everyday lives. Whether rich or poor, a housewife or a workaholic, a go-getter or some computer nerd who thrives on making money online, everyone unknowingly expresses some form of ambition on a daily basis.

These daily acts of ambition are easy, but they are difficult to recognize, as they have blended in with our daily habits, goals, schedules, chores, home works, and to-do lists.

Our ambition, when mixed with positive habits, can be very productive in every avenue of our lives, from our careers to our relationships and even in business, not to mention personal growth. Most of us recognize the good habits we pick up on, do them over and over, and are very much aware of our productivity, but we seldom pick up on the ambitious aspect of it. It is one of the secret driving forces that help us persevere and develop productive habits in order to reach our expected goal.

Habits can be good or bad. They can either lead you to failure or play a major role in your success. Most of the time, when we do develop good habits, we subconsciously miss the part when we have the drive, tenacity, zeal, vision, motivation, and much more. We hardly notice the fact that these attributes derive from the secret ambition within us. And yet we scorn the thought of ambition when one mentions it.

We set goals every day—goals for our families, goals for our friends, goals for our businesses, and most importantly, goals for ourselves—and yet we do not realize that without a little ambition, most goals would be impossible to complete. If you ask someone who indulges in mediocrity and has accepted the negative aspects of ambition, they might say, *"Money is the root of all evil."* And they will say, *"It's not always about money."*

The truth is that some folks in mediocrity will scorn the thought of ambition, not because they think it's bad, but because it reminds them of their failures, and the fact that they have no plans, goals, or dreams. And even if they do, they are not doing anything about them, and so make assumptions that anyone with ambition is someone who's chasing after money, which is not always so. The act of scorning ambition, or those who act upon it, makes them feel better about the *stagnant* state they are in. I'm *not* suggesting that everyone in mediocrity feels that way. I want to stress that point. But there *are* those who say such things. When you ask someone who has been successful at something, or is still pursuing something and developing their ambition, they will often say, *"My desire is not strong enough; I need to push harder."* They feel this way despite the fact that their efforts are already bearing some kind of fruit. That is so because the mindset of an ambitious person is such that, no matter how much fruit they bear, they will never be satisfied until they reach their expected goal. More often than not, their plans, goals, and daily agendas are so full that, once they accomplish a task, they jump right onto the next one, focusing on their dreams and what they need to become in life. That is the ultimate prize.

Why do we wake up early every morning and make schedules, do chores, and perform work around the house? It is because our human nature has the desire to get things done. This is basic ambition at its best. So when this aspect of human nature is applied to a bigger goal, bigger plans, bigger dreams, or even bigger achievements, it leaves the stage of basic ambition, and is elevated to the form of ambition that has been utilized by inventors, artists, entrepreneurs, scholars, and leaders in general, throughout the ages.

We express basic forms of ambition with our families, building family businesses, working on goals for our children, and focusing on building fine relationships with our spouses, children, relatives, and even neighbors. In these cases, though not perfect, we work on our loyalty, trust, and reliability, which also automatically follow us into our jobs and careers.

In sports, basic ambition can easily evolve from simply developing positive daily habits to a level of extraordinary greatness. I know a story about a man named Michael Jordan (you might have heard of him). It began in a place called Wilmington, North Carolina. From his early years, MJ's competitiveness with his siblings and those around him always challenged him to be better than his current state. Basic small ambitions, which he developed in his younger years, followed him throughout his amazing career. Let me explain. Many do not know that, in high school, MJ tried out for his varsity basketball team during his sophomore year, but because he was 5'11", he was deemed too short to play at that level. He could have called it quits at that point, but he was too ambitious to do that, and his competitive nature would not permit him to do so. He had developed a habit of persistence. He always just kept on going. Though he was not yet qualified at that level of play, he decided that he would work harder in order to make himself qualified.

Motivated to prove his self-worth, MJ became the star of Laney's junior varsity squad, pulling off several forty-point games. The following summer, he grew four inches and trained even harder. After earning a spot on the varsity roster, MJ averaged about twenty points per game over his final two seasons. By his senior year, he was selected to the McDonald's All-American Team, after averaging a triple-double. Then he received a basketball scholarship to North Carolina.

But the drive and basic ambition that he developed in his younger years did not stop there for MJ. It followed him to the NBA, where he was picked third overall by the Chicago Bulls. He quickly became a fan favorite in the NBA, averaging twenty-eight points a game and was recognized by magazines like *Sports Illustrated*. Just over a month into his professional career, headlines declared that *"A star is born."*

In the beginning of his NBA career, MJ faced many obstacles. Other players were jealous. He also broke his foot in his second season, causing him to miss sixty-four games, many of which his teammates were unable to win. Despite all of these hindrances and his injury, he was able to bounce back and his team made it to the playoffs that year, where he set a new record for points scored in a playoff game (63), an achievement that's still unbroken. He went on to win six NBA championships and multiple other awards and honors, like being named the NBA finals' MVP, as well as the NBA's MVP multiple times.

It seemed like the basic ambition he developed as a boy was working out quite well for him, so it was impossible to stop there. After his retirement, he bought a minority stake in the Charlotte Bobcats, and became the team's second-largest owner behind the majority owner. About a decade later, he went on to be the majority owner of the NBA team.

MJ's marked talent was apparent from his earlier years on the court, but one can't help but accept the fact that his positive basic daily ambitions throughout his life have made him one of the most prolific names in sports, even long after his retirement, and earned him the title of *"the greatest basketball player of all time."* In 1999, ESPN ranked him the greatest North American athlete of the twentieth century. And it all began with the small, basic, almost-invisible steps of ambition, which he took in his small home in Wilmington, North Carolina.

As a member of the church as a whole, I've witnessed some ministers, pastors, bishops, and so on become very productive in their personal lives and communities, while others have not. It doesn't mean that one is better than the other, and it can't be dismissed as simple differences in denominations. If you travel a few years back in their lives, you'll quickly find out why some are productive and some are not. Basic small goals or dreams, worked on at a very young age, have over time brought some of them great dividends, and touched the lives of people all across the nation on a very vast scale.

As for those who are not as successful or productive in the same way, they have depended on customs, systems, and man-made rules (including traditions) to set their goals for them. This, in turn, leaves them in the same place that their predecessors or mentors left off. Secretly, ambition is already hidden in the hearts of men, and has been throughout the ages. We have seen it demonstrated all around us, for the desire to become something or achieve something in their lives is in every human soul, big or small, rich or poor. I once observed a young child trying to build a Lego house in front of his father. After every Lego that he connected together, he would happily look at his father, rejoicing and throwing his hands up in the air in recognition of his achievement. To him, *every single piece* was worthy of celebration. This attribute doesn't change too much when we get older. Though sometimes hardly noticed, the desire to achieve something shows itself in our relationships, careers, education, and even businesses.

Note: The human will to become something is similar to a flowing river; as long as there is a journey, it will keep on moving.

Sometimes, people who scorn ambition (though they have it) try to give it a different name, for negative reasons. They hide their ambition, because everything around them (including people) have defined ambition as a bad thing. They will use terms like perseverance, determination, tenacity, being strong-willed, a go-getter, or a self-motivator. But it would help a lot of people if they would just call it what it is: ambition. They are after something. They are ambitious. And that is a good thing.

Throughout history, we have seen inventors like the Wright brothers, Thomas Edison, Alexander Graham Bell, Leonardo da Vinci, James Watt, Albert Einstein, Henry Ford, Steve Jobs, Isaac Newton, Garrett Morgan,

Benjamin Franklin, Nikola Tesla, and *so* many more, all driven by their ambitions to do something much greater than what they saw around them. Their inventions are still very much with us to this day. Nations all across the world have benefited from these men's persistence to do something far beyond the ordinary, placing them on the world stage even long after their deaths. Humanity does not like to be unproductive. That is just a fact. The difference between those who are stagnant and those who are persevering is that the one chooses to do something about "it" while the other is waiting for handouts. Life seems like it's never fair at times, but it's never partial, either; we all have what it takes to achieve something. The question is whether we want it badly enough, or whether we are willing to follow good advice and do whatever it takes to be our best us.

Opportunities seldom come our way, and when they do, it's usually when we least expect it. The minority who are alert to the possibilities and always anticipate them tend to respond much more quickly. Unfortunately, most people miss them completely. It is very rare to see someone with a productive attitude fail in life. If they are not successful in business, they will be in relationships. If they are not successful at school, they tend to create or invent something. These positive attitudes come mostly from basic small ambitions that have been worked on and which, over time, evolve into an intrinsic drive to never stop moving and never settle for failure.

CHAPTER 4
THE SILENT GIANT

I know a young man who wanted only to "be something" in life. He did not finish college, had no profession, and no career. All he had was his will. All odds were against him. He could have come up with every excuse he could imagine, but instead, he just kept on going. He filled out one job application after another. He worked cleaning ditches, sorting garbage, cleaning parking lots, and shoveling snow. For over ten years, he did just about every odd job you could think of. Despite the mockery from employers, the lack of support, the humiliation and workplace abuse, and being made to do all the extra labor that no one else would do, he persevered.

He always used to say, *"There's got to be more to life than this."* Though his current circumstance was nothing but doom and gloom, he refused to see or accept it. Moving from job to job, city to city, and apartment to apartments (at times even getting evicted for not being able to pay his rent), it seemed like life would never be stable for this young man. But as he persevered, and as the years went by, he began to realize that *focusing on what was on the outside could not detract from what had been forming within him.*

He began to realize that there was much more to him than could be seen from the outside. Sensing that something was happening within him, he began to realize that his experiences and afflictions in life were just tools to awaken a sleeping giant within him, consisting of gifts and skills that would not just help him become financially free but also help millions of people find their paths, as well. He began to learn how to embrace his experiences and afflictions, and even challenged himself by setting higher goals. He began to think much more of himself than what his current state was telling him.

After years of turmoil and confusion, he was able to write a book that was birthed from the same experiences and afflictions he had thought were destroying his life. The book became a *New York Times* bestseller, and the doors that had once seemed shut to him were opened wide. His experiences and afflictions that had seemed like a curse for so long became his education and a source of life. The young man who had been sorting garbage and cleaning ditches became a millionaire, and a very influential individual in his country and nations across the world.

I told this story in the hopes of helping you to understand where I am trying to go in this chapter. We humans have the tendency to try to avoid afflictions or bad experiences as much as we can. We cringe at the thought of them, and in most cases, we become consumed with fear and worry at their very idea. What an individual who is trying to become something in life has to understand and accept is that afflictions, trials, and bad experiences are going to come anyway. They are inevitable.

Champions are not made or formed walking through parks or taking vacations away from society into the cocoon islands. Champions are born when all hell has broken loose in their life, and rather than fleeing, they stand tall in the midst of the darkness surrounding them, persevering and eventually overcoming the obstacles.

Society has taught us many things, and most of what we've learned has crippled our ability to become all that we can be. We are living in a world that has contaminated and demonized one of the things that can release the greatest treasures within us. We are so focused and distracted by what our eyes can see, trying to make life as comfortable as possible. Being comfortable is not wrong, but expecting to start off that way is.

In every human being, there are gifts and treasures that just need to be revealed, and most times, it is the afflictions and challenges that do that. These treasures, which I nicknamed "the sleeping giant," can vary. Every individual is unique, and every individual has something in them that cannot be copied or imitated. We have abilities within us that can change nations, communities, and even whole generations.

Note: Affliction in a human's life is like dirty soil; without it, the seed will never grow.

Note: Human abilities are similar to a tree in its seed stage; if you don't water and tend to it, it won't grow.

They say God's most unique creation is the human being. I agree. As I have already explained, it consists of three entities: the spirit, the soul, and the body. The body, which we see, does all the dirty work. The soul, which is the mediator between the two others, contains our emotions, personalities, and so on. The spirit is where all our gifts and supernatural greatness dwells. Most times, we ignore our spirit, and its true essence, which I will elaborate on in the next chapter. Our fight is really between two entities: our spirit and our body. The body, which is fleshly, is the least and most destructive of the three; it was never created to be the lead entity. The spirit was to take that role, for in the spirit lies our greatest potential.

We live in a world that has taught us to listen to the urges and desires of our bodies, and sadly, in most cases, that doesn't end too well. The human body is similar to a baby; it will take anything you give it, even if it's bad for it. The body wasn't created to discern what is good or bad for it. It was created to be the hands and feet with which one's purpose on earth can be fulfilled. The body is loud and arrogant, always wanting to take part in pleasure and fleshly activities that often hinder any kind of growth or productivity. The flesh or body, focusing on what pleases it the most, develops things like anger, resentment, hate, un-forgiveness, loneliness, low self-esteem, lust, greed, and more. All these do nothing but keep the spirit within you in a prison. That is why people remain in poverty, always wanting or needy, lost and lacking identity, always eager to fit in with whatever is presented to them.

It is then necessary that life takes us through rough roads, difficult circumstances, storms, and trenches. Afflictions or challenges in life have a way of humbling us, and helping us to make better decisions. They have a way of setting us free from all the heaviness and weight that our fleshly nature has acquired. These moments of our life can be very dark and sometimes very difficult to bear. The silent giant within us is searching for a way out, but, sadly, we continue to put ourselves in situations and circumstances that keep us stuck. We tend to remain in our afflictions far longer than we are supposed to, because our human nature cannot grasp what it is trying to accomplish. It is trying to help us develop attributes and characteristics that, when applied and observed, will (over time) awaken the greater person (giant) within us. It saddens me to see people struggle with difficult times, live unstable lives, and stay stuck in the same place they were five years ago. It is usually because they believe in the same system or protocols that *keep* them in the same place: the same attitude, views, and personalities. The same state of mind.

Note: No one knows the heart and character of a man until it's revealed through fire.

When life is good, and all is going well, you rarely see an individual examine themselves to see what kind of attitudes and characteristics they need to work on to become a better person. However, the majority of those who are going through some form of struggle in their lives can be found reading books, going to seminars, joining programs for character-building, and much more, because they are constantly looking for the means to change and better their lives. They generally do not realize or notice that it is during this dark time that they develop patience, humility, and other characteristics that will draw people to them rather than push them away, while also getting rid of all the weight of the negative attributes they have been carrying for years. This process, in return, will automatically open the prison door, releasing the giant within you and allowing your gifts, talents, and unique abilities to be free.

Pain is temporary, but quitting lasts forever. People quit on their dreams and choose to accept life's worst moments because most don't realize that every one of us has the potential to be masters at what we do.

Unfortunately, the truth is that most of us just don't believe this truth . . . but beliefs are nothing but personal perceptions we've carried from our youth. They become our personal truths, but that doesn't mean that they are facts. The fact is that, whatever it is you are going through, you are not going through it if you're not built to overcome it!

Our beliefs, whether good or bad, will determine our behaviors and reaction to life's difficult times. We really have only two options with anything that life throws at us: We can either quit and/or accept failure; or keep on pushing, whether we fail or not, subconsciously exercising the giant within us.

Our very best is not revealed or challenged when all is going well and everything is champagne and strawberries. No. Our very best is challenged when it's provoked by the storms and darkest moments that life throws at us. People seldom realize that they are the masters of their own fate, and that every decision they make, in every area of their lives, is critical. But it is the truth.

Knowing this, we must learn to minimize mistakes as much as possible, and stay ever alert, ready to take advantage of every opportunity that might take us a step closer to our God-given purpose. Every individual is responsible for themselves. Looking at ourselves in the mirror and having pity for ourselves is not going to change our situations, but taking even one step toward our goals might—and is a lot more productive than taking no steps at all.

Humans have the tendency to forget who they really are when all hell is breaking loose in their lives. They have bought into the false ideologies that people and surroundings have taught them. In some cases, they have been in the workforce for so long, holding onto a low-paying job and settling for the least-respected positions, that they have forgotten about their true potential and genius within them.

The same sort of settling and forgetfulness is in play within intimate relationships, friendships, and families. Past events, moments, and failures in any of these areas have a way of choking any new type of life that is trying to take shape in your present and future. This lack of awareness of all that the people in their lives and surroundings have taught them has unguardedly allowed them to adopt a perception of themselves that others have embraced, pushing the giant within themselves down even deeper.

It is inevitable that our thought processes will determine our results in this difficult world we live in. *One should not jump out of the boat and into the vast ocean until their mindset is capable of handling the sharks (obstacles) lurking all around, waiting to devour us the moment we hit the water.*

What do I mean by this? Our thought processes and belief systems, in dealing with life's obstacles and challenges, are so important that, if exercised correctly, they have the power to elevate us to levels of greatness we never thought we could reach. On the other hand, if our state of mind is not ready for the ocean, it will cause us to sink into mediocrity, and eventually, a life of unproductivity.

I have a problem watching people give in too soon to life's obstacles, throwing in the towel and turning back, just because they think they are not getting anywhere. We must learn to accept that *focus combined with patience can lead us to great victories in life.* When we encounter some difficult moments, we tend to take a step back and lose our focus. Done repeatedly, this has a way of luring us into going after daily pursuits that are no more than distractions from our original goals.

Note: A focused mind mixed with great zeal is the recipe for producing countless victories.

Most people fall away and quit pursuing the goals they have set for themselves because they become weary of the journey. We live in a microwave world that demands everything happen right away. What we should know is that a sleeping giant can't be woken up with whispers and a little shake; it has to be done with kicks and thunderstorms, and like any human who is just getting out of bed, it will take some time for them to come fully back to consciousness.

We never achieve the goals we set for ourselves when our commitment is not level with our focus. Focus with zeal is what differentiates the winners from the losers. While others are partying, great athletes are training. While others are watching television, great athletes are watching tapes. While others are sleeping, great athletes are staying up late and getting up early, working on their skill sets. As such, it is no surprise that they achieve the things they achieve. These great athletes focus relentlessly on what makes them better, for years, until it becomes effortless. That is what makes them champions.

> Note: A champion ain't no champion until they have defeated every attack against them.

CHAPTER 5
HIDDEN POTENTIAL

Note: The most unique creations on earth are the ones who were created to nourish it: humans.

There is more to the human race than one could actually comprehend. There are treasures hidden so deep within us that most do not realize they are there. We get so caught up in other people's opinions of us that we fail to see the riches that lie within. No one can be you but you. So then, if that value in you is not brought forth, you have robbed the earth of its true glory. The earth and everything it contains are counting on your abilities and skill set to nourish them, whether through people or with nature.

The most important thing to realize is how the earth benefits when individuals realize the greatness in them and allow it to flourish, within the surroundings in which they are placed. We, as humans, are very prone to looking everywhere else to find some sense of belonging, when in truth, all the identity and belonging we need is within us. We spend more time studying other things than we do ourselves. If people could spend half the time and energy they focus on things of no value searching their inner selves, we would discover things about ourselves that money can't buy.

People always work so hard to try to prove themselves to others, when in truth, it's just because they haven't seen the value in themselves. Trying to impress their boss, neighbors, pastors, friends. . . . They do all this in order to get some level of approval and sense of assurance. Because they do not have fulfillment in their lives, they look for attention and status anywhere they can find it. Those questionable sources vary, but by getting assurance and a sense of approval from people whom they only assume are fulfilled, they hope to get a small part of that fulfillment for themselves. You can follow the wisest people, be around the most famous people, attend the best seminars, but if you've not recognized the value in yourself, then all your efforts will be in vain. Understanding our own hidden potential is the best discovery one could make in their lifetime. There is a story I always tell, and thought it would be appropriate at this time: the story about the eagle amongst common birds:

> *There was once a baby eagle that lived amongst common birds. Growing up amongst them was all that it knew. So, whatever those birds did, it would do the same. It would fly as high as they flew, eat as they ate, flap its wings as they did, and move as they moved. It became what its surroundings had introduced it to. Its beliefs and perception of itself were that of a common bird.*

> *But as time went on, living as those birds did was starting to take a toll on it. It was getting hungrier, because it needed to eat more. It was considered different. The common birds never wanted it near them, because they found it to be weird. It became the laughing stock of the bird colony. Then one day, after a long string of incidents full of turmoil, it had had enough!*

> *It took its eyes off everyone else and began to look toward itself. It noticed that its wings were bigger, its beak stronger, its body broader, and its legs much bigger than those of the other birds. Its stature far exceeded theirs. It then chose*

to get out of its smaller surroundings and exercise what it had just discovered about itself.

It walked to the cliff's edge, and, though fearful and not knowing what might happen, it cast itself into the open air, instinctively stretched out its wings, and began to soar. The more time it spent in the air, the more it realized that this was where it belonged. It was built to soar.

Realizing this, the eagle flew higher and higher. It had discovered its true surroundings and what it was born to be. And so it was that the eagle, who once thought it was a common bird, realized that its potential was much greater than it had ever dreamed.

If the cares of life have accomplished anything throughout the ages, it is making us think far less of ourselves than we really ought to.

Note: Greatness, when it is searched for, is like a turtle believing that it can move faster on dry ground than in the water.

People, in most cases, do not realize that there are two voices fighting within them at all times. One wants to help them be all that they can be; the other would stop at nothing to see them fail. The voice that wins is the one the individual chooses to listen to the most. This is an ongoing battle within us, and if one doesn't act wisely, choosing the proper voice to listen to, the pitfalls can be so great it can be almost impossible to climb back out.

As I have alluded to before, the hidden potential within us is very similar to a tree; if you stop watering or tending to it after seeing it sprout a little from the ground, it won't take long before you see it die, robbed of the opportunity to ever reach its fullest potential. Every man is responsible for themselves first, before they are qualified to be responsible for others. Being responsible for others can be no more than simply helping people to discover who they are so that they can take their rightful place in life, which was given to them before the foundation of the world. So, if you haven't discovered who you are, how can you help someone else discover who they are?

Note: The path to self-discovery is so full of riches it would leave the carrier overwhelmed with what they find.

And now, I believe that it is only right for me to dive more deeply into the hidden human potential that lurks deep within us.

Note: There is no treasure that one can receive in life that is more equipped and full of unexplained gifts than that which is already in them: the human spirit.

Not knowing the basic teachings of who we are as humans tends to lure us much further away from what we are called to be. I hear people talk about important things like goals, dreams, opportunities, and aspirations, but none is more important or worth talking about than the human spirit. It is the essence of our true nature and the storekeeper of our identity. Every human owes it to themselves to observe and search for their inner-self: their spirit. Within it are answers one cannot find anywhere else. We can find courage, perseverance, hope, love, and confidence in this human entity that is rarely spoken of in this day and age.

The bible teaches us that, first, God made the body, but the body was dead, so God blew His spirit (life) into the body (flesh), and the body became a living soul. What can we learn from this? Without the spirit, the body has no value, and it is of no importance. As the spirit was blown into the body, it contained all the gifts and attributes of the man as a whole. So then, if the earth is in a natural realm, and the spirit is in a supernatural realm, in order for the spirit to be able to function on earth, it requires a body. The body is similar to a container, which has no value if there is nothing within it. The spirit came with life and a task to be fulfilled, and the body is the container that helps it address the task at hand. Both need each other; the body without the spirit is no more than a useless container, and the spirit without the body is just an entity full of potential with no body through which it may express its greatness. The spirit wasn't designed to be subject to the body, but the body *is* to be subject to the spirit. We live in a world where people unknowingly allow their bodies to lead, when that ought not to be so. Hence, the world is what it is today: divided, dangerous, confused, and full of uncertainty. We have allowed the container that was once empty to lead the one with the agenda: the spirit. The spirit will never agree with the waywardness of the body, and the body is too consumed with its frail human nature to be subjected to the spirit; hence, the fight begins, borne of not knowing who we are and the thirst to discover our identity.

Our soul, which is the mediator between the two, is mostly confused about from whom it should take information. When the spirit is telling it that it's great, the body says it's mediocre. When the spirit says that it's important, the body says it's worthless. When the spirit says that it's rich, the body says it's poor. And when the spirit says that there is great potential within it, the body says it is nothing more than what its present situation is telling it.

These are some of the reasons why our body, or our fleshly nature, was never created to lead, but people have a tendency to heed their fleshly nature more than their spirit. Most people who have become champions in any avenue of life, whether it be in business, sports, ministry, government, personal growth, and so on, have learned how to listen to their spirit, their inner-selves, one way or another, whether they realize it or not.

Note: Many will stand on the brink of success, but the man who is one with his spirit will fly right over.

Being connected to our spirit is one of the most important things we can do. It is our peace in turmoil, our hope in uncertainty, our strength in weakness, our light in darkness, our sight in unseen territories, and our comfort in time of need. It can mend hearts that are broken, heal deep wounds within our hearts, and erase the scars left behind by the cares of life. We need not live a life of searching or wanting if we are connected to our inner-selves. As the human being is three entities in one, when all are in agreement, we can accomplish things that seem impossible. We see many people who live lives that seem very unattractive to most of us; others live lives that are dysfunctional and out of order, and rather than searching themselves and beginning a process of personal development, they sometimes—sadly—choose to remain in the pit that they have sub-consciously dug for themselves.

But time waits for no one. Neither is it slowing down nor getting old. The only one who's getting old is you, and it is best to get old with wisdom and a better understanding of who we are, growing every day.

I have a great friend, one whom I trust and with whom I am very close. He embodies the point I am trying to make. What he was when he allowed his body (flesh) to lead his life, and who he is today, now that his spirit has been given the lead, could not be more different. He lived a very unfortunate life. Having grown up in circumstances he never created and was not responsible for, he was confused, misled, and even failed in many things. It wasn't long before the young man began to allow his flesh to get the best of him. Misguided and alone, lost with no sense of identity, he sought gangs to affiliate himself with, relationships to find comfort in, fights to prove his self-worth, and drugs to sell for money, survival, and some sense of importance. The majority of his teenage life was spent in homeless shelters, sleeping on park benches, in central police stations, and even prisons.

He adopted the teachings of the church in his early twenties and a drastic change quickly began to take place in his life. His habits began to change, his belief system began to be established, positive characteristics began to form in him, and his attitude and perception of himself became positive. He realized that he was more valuable than his past had led him to believe. Best of all, his identity began to reveal itself.

Since that day of self-discovery when he recognized and accepted his inner-man, every decision he makes, whether small or great, now pertains to who he was born to be: a champion for himself and others! With that new belief and understanding of himself, that young man went on to become an influential individual in his community, and a role model to the generation coming after him.

The spirit in man, at its core, is an entity that was designed to use the body to beautify the earth and its inhabitants, but when our human nature or our fleshly characteristics come into play, the spirit—though never turning completely away from its original agenda—instinctively takes on another responsibility: helping us to overcome all the obstacles and hardships life has thrown at us. These obstacles are often ones we place in our own paths. Emotional hurts, pride, and self-inflicted wounds lead to anger, hatred, discord, and confusion, with an unending list of negative characteristics. All these things, and so much more, play a major role in our shortcomings and failures.

The spirit man within us, when exercised, is an underrated doctor that can heal us of all of these things and replace them with joy, fulfillment, satisfaction, confidence, belief, hope, trust, and the most important thing of all: love. It saturates us with its soothing revelation day after day, and gives us a better understanding of a hopeful tomorrow, even in times of darkness and doubt.

A good friend of mine once told me that it is difficult for most people to think there is a better tomorrow when they don't think that they will be a part of it. Your spirit will help you realize that you are a candidate for and a participant in a better tomorrow, despite who you are, where you come from, or where you've been. It doesn't matter. You are unique and wonderful and perfect in the master's eyes.

Note: Treasures within are not treasures if they are not discovered and put to use.

I remember the late Dr. Myles Monroe, who was a man of great wisdom and respect whom I had grown to admire and regard very highly. He said, *"The richest place on earth is not the oil sands of Saudi Arabia. The richest place on earth is not Wall Street or Main Street. And the richest place on earth is not the diamond lands of Africa. The richest place on earth is the cemetery!"* I was troubled and confused as I pondered this statement, until I heard what he said next, which changed my perception of life forever. He said, *"Because in the cemetery lay songs that were never written, businesses that were never opened, talents and gifts that were never exercised, books that were never written, ministries that were never established, and dreams that were never fulfilled."*

Why? Because people live all their lives in procrastination, emptiness, mediocrity, doubt, and low self-esteem, not striving to be all that they could be but choosing to bury their gifts with them in failure. As they had buried their gifts while they were alive, those same gifts were buried with them six feet under. With no one to speak of them, no legacy to leave behind, and blessing no one, they died with the weight of their gifts and talents within them, instead of going to their graves light, unencumbered by all the gifts with which they were born.

These gifts and talents were designed to be left behind for those who are alive to grow and be blessed by them. The saddest moment in life is when one is on their death bed looking back at their life, realizing that they have left nothing behind that has value. They wish that they could have some more time, but, sadly, they can't; they quietly die in sorrow and regret, with the knowledge that they are dying with the same gifts and potential that they were born with, and have to conclude that they lived a life with no meaning.

Note: Potential unrealized is like a caterpillar that thinks its current state is the most beautiful stage of its existence.

Life can be so full of joy if we do not allow our fleshly nature to have control of our lives but, rather, reap the benefits of allowing our inner-man and spirit to lead our lives. The entities and design of humans are really simple and what distinguish us from animals and any other creature. We were made with body, soul, and spirit. The way these three entities function is unique and impossible for us to truly understand. The spirit has all the information, gifts, and abilities; it gives our soul these tools and strategies, conveying how it ought to be accomplished, and then the soul directs this information to the body, which then fulfills the spiritual agenda in the natural realm that we know.

Talk about creation at its best. The human being is our creator's greatest handiwork! We are so valuable that the bible teaches us that, after sin or different forms of dysfunctions enters our hearts, it contaminates us and shuts down every good thing in us. It is thought that the creator himself took on human flesh, and paid a price for our dysfunctions, restoring unto us that which we had lost. And so, once again, we are in a position to be the best that we can be through Him, just as He had intended it to be from the beginning, being excellent in everything we do and doing it all with perfection.

Whether you believe in this truth or not, one thing is sure: No one has an excuse for not striving to be all that they could be.

Observing nature, I can't help but ask myself questions. Can the leaves of trees make such beautiful sounds without the force of the wind? Can the ocean make waves without the shore? Can the open sky be the same without the splendor of the clouds and stars? With that said, neither can our human body reach its fullest potential without the spirit.

Note: The spirit-and-body combination is similar to a moving car and its driver; without the driver, the car is just an accident waiting to happen.

Though it is a good thing, we must come to a place of realization where we know that our self-worth is not measured by how much we achieve but by the treasures we contain. There are great opportunities and things in life that we miss—not because we want to, but because we do not know what we are destined to be. As such, we were not mentally awake to what was presented to us.

The key to life is not jumping from one place to another, one relationship to another, one idea to another, one goal to another, and never accomplishing anything. The key to life is discovering who we are in order to be the best at everything that comes our way at any point of our lives. Whatever you come across in life, whether in terms of opportunities, relationships, ministries, businesses, or anything else, you will do it to the best of your hidden abilities, blessing yourself, and, more importantly, blessing those who will be affected by your efforts. *For success is a beautiful thing, but success is not measured by how much money you have, but how much of your own God-given abilities you've exercised in order for you to be a blessing to somebody else.*

Life is short, no matter how old we get. Why? Because whether we like it or not, we are going to die one day. As such, it is best that every blessed moment we live be spent striving to achieve something positive toward our life's purpose, whether internally or externally.

The purpose of man is of such value and importance that, if even one soul dies without fulfilling its destiny, it would be very difficult to replace, because every other soul is already occupied with their own. We are the best of ourselves, and no one is able to do what you do the way you do it.

I have noticed that, in Hollywood, every time they want to make a movie based on a true story, they will interview the individual on whom that movie will be based. They will also speak to family members and friends of the individual, and will even go so far as allowing the actor who is going to portray the individual to spend a lot of time with them. Many of these movies turn out to be really good, with the help of good directors and actors. But one thing I realize, after the movie, is that no matter how many times they interviewed and investigated the individual, and regardless of how much time they allowed the actor to spend with them, they never get it perfect. The individual on whom the story is based is very unique in a way that can never be recreated. That is a fact!

Nelson Mandela once said, *"I am the master of my own fate and the champion of my soul."* There are many ways one can interpret this powerful statement, and it fits with the point I am trying to make. I could interpret this to mean that no one has the responsibility (or what it takes) to bring out the best in you; the only one who can do that is you, since no one can go inside of another and bring forth their hidden treasures or potential. This is what makes you the master of your fate and champion of your soul.

This is the greatest victory that one must strive to achieve. Some will say, "But we need other people to help us be the best that we can be." I agree. But we must also realize that people—whether family, friends, scholars, writers, singers, or motivational speakers—can only show us the direction and give us the fundamental tools and ideas to stir up the greatness within us that will facilitate our own great exploits in life.

CHAPTER 6
THE CURSE OF MEDIOCRITY

Note: Many challenges are thrown at us daily, but mediocrity is what we throw at ourselves.

Note: There are many blessings given to the human race, but mediocrity is not one of them.

Out of all the chapters in this book, this is probably the most important, or at least right up there in my top five. Why do I say that? It is very hard to show someone the truth when they have been brought up to believe in falsehoods. Mediocrity is like addiction—once you take a hit of it, you can't stop taking it, even though you know very well it's bad for you. Mediocrity to the human soul is no different than snake poison to the human body; once you've been bit, it's only a matter of time before it consumes the whole body and leads to death.

It is like repeatedly taking counsel from someone who's satisfied with being average; after a while, you become that which you've been listening to: average. Now there are some who are average but doing very well within their circle, whether it be with their careers, relationships, or anything else. I am not speaking of those, for not all who are living an average life are stuck in the state of mind of stagnancy.

Now, back to the point I'm trying to emphasize on mediocrity: It is no different than standing outside, looking at a beautifully decorated store, but when you go inside to purchase something, you find it totally empty. *No one* who has overcome this human curse can even imagine what would the world be like if we all stepped out of mediocrity and into lives lived with purpose and meaning.

Growing up, I had the privilege of witnessing some terrible things around me that affected me emotionally, physically, and financially. You might ask, "Then why was it a privilege?" Well, the answer is very simple: If I had not experienced or seen the terrible effects of negativity, I would have never realized how bad it was for my future aspirations. Everyone has the right to choose whether they want to remain in a state of mediocrity or make positive decisions that might give them a fighting chance of accomplishing amazing goals in life. I have lived in neighborhoods full of poverty, violence of all sorts, broken-down buildings, crack houses, homelessness, chains on the doors of stores that had gone out of business—areas where constant negativity was the norm. Sadly, only a very small few make it out there alive, whether that means dying physically or spiritually—either way, they are not really alive. They live as the walking dead.

I have lost amazing friends and people to physical deaths, people whom most folks would call worthless, thugs who were up to no good. "It was their fate." I find it very difficult to come to that conclusion, for I knew most of them personally. They loved their families, were full of joy and laughter, and were amazing characters, at times the life of the party. It is always a sad reality for me, watching all those good characteristics in people capable of great achievements, and seeing it all buried six feet under. I have seen single mothers work countless hours to provide for their children, fathers living lives so negative that they do not even notice their child is taking up right after them.

This is not the case for everyone. There are also those who choose to find ordinary jobs, knowing they are capable of much more, and stay there for years in that same state, not striving or believing that life can get any better, satisfied with making minimum wage or just enough to get by. I have seen bad habits lead to people continuing living a life of being average—a life subconsciously passed on from generation to generation—and yet not many people in their surroundings could notice. I have lived in neighborhoods where success is only for Hollywood stars, big business owners, CEOs, doctors, government officials, and those of great influence in every avenue of life.

How did I come out of mediocrity? When I began to realize that I wanted my life to be much more than just living day by day, just getting by, that realization left me open to receiving or discovering opportunities that would help me get out of that way of living.

It is strange when I hear people speak as if there is nothing out there—no hope, no opportunities, no growth, no future. At this stage in life, the difference between people who are successful and those who are not is that the former will go out there and take their chance. The unique thing about people of such zeal is that, even if they do not see or discover any opportunities, they will create their own. This is unlike the people who say there is nothing out there, and who choose to do nothing about it—people who have accepted failure, and embraced mediocrity, and then wait as they reap the results of that decision, which weighs them down with stress, anger, resentment, low self-esteem, depression, and so much more.

People like myself, who are trying to accomplish something in life or are striving to do so, have one thing in common: *Failure is not an option!*

People have allowed the system of mediocrity to be embedded so deeply within themselves that it has taking over every decision they make in every avenue of their lives. This ultimately will allow the curse of a particular surrounding or circumstance to be a curse unto themselves and future generations.

The definition of a curse is the expression of a wish that misfortune, evil, or doom will befall a person or a group. That is what mediocrity has done throughout history, and it is still doing it, contaminating the hearts of men.

There are multiple differences between those who are striving to be something in life and those who are under a curse of mediocrity:

* Goal-oriented people "read daily"; mediocre people "watch TV daily."
* Goal-oriented people "set goals"; mediocre people "never set goals."
* Goal-oriented people "compliment others"; mediocre people "criticize others."
* Goal-oriented people "embrace change"; mediocre people "fear change."
* Goal-oriented people "forgive"; mediocre people "hold grudges."
* Goal-oriented people "talk about ideas"; mediocre people "talk about people."
* Goal-oriented people "continuously learn"; mediocre people "think they know it all."
* Goal-oriented people take responsibility for their failures; mediocre people "blame others for their failures."

Mediocrity in communities

There is an old saying: *"Monkey see, monkey do."* No parent wants their child to live a life of insufficiency and lack. They do the best they can by putting them through kindergarten, elementary, high school, and even college, if they make it that far. What happens along the way, as their child's character begins to change and adapt to what they have been introduced to? Their child's associations—the friends that they keep in the neighborhoods that they live in—will start to play a role in their lives. If they are individuals who possess good personalities and attributes, it will eventually lead them to success; if they don't pick up on those qualities quickly, when in negative surroundings they will think that they need to change in order to fit in with this new group of people. This can happen in elementary school, high school, college, or just with all those around them in general, from family to co-workers.

Parents make one of their biggest mistakes when they wait to start teaching their children about life's difficulties and challenges until they are in high school or grown up. These parents now put themselves in a tug of war between themselves and their children's circle of influence. Most times, the children leave, and so the cycle continues, just like the curse that has plagued society for generations: lives lived without purpose.

In worst cases, parents don't know how to teach their children to strive for greatness, or how to make the decisions pertaining to that. How could they? They themselves were never taught it, and so were never aware of it. Most parents assume that making sure that their children have food to eat and a place to sleep is the only job they have in raising them. This is a problem that has destroyed communities and buried the gifts of young lives that will possibly never have the chance to discover the greatness that lurks within them.

In most communities, they teach that you go to school, get a job, get married, and raise a family. And in a way, there is nothing wrong with that. There are critical life lessons along that journey that one should adopt, learn from, and, best of all, grow as a person as a result of. The problem is that there is much more to every individual's life than just going to school and getting a job. It is important to go through life always looking for the means to discover things about yourself that can give you the mental, emotional, physical, financial, and even spiritual freedom you deserve, coming out of the prison of the masses. So, as you go through school, work, or any other adventure in which you find yourself, it is very important to allow these experiences and journeys to reveal something about yourself that you never thought you had. Sadly, this important life principle is never taught in most communities. We go through life just hoping to get by, when, in truth, almost every situation, experience, circumstance, or event that occurred or is occurring in one's life is supposed to help us get closer to self-discovery and understanding. This is vital, or else nothing that we go through is really of any importance. We suffered for nothing. The moments when we find gems within us that we could never find in schools, jobs, or anywhere else are incredibly pivotal.

I love the thought of success. Though I hated some of the situations and circumstances of my childhood, I am glad they happened because every circumstance was a learning curve in my life, whether young or old. Because I never had materialistic things, I wanted to get myself to a place where I could get them. Because I never had a stable home growing up, I wanted to create one. Because I never had enough food, I wanted to live a life where I could afford sufficient sustenance. Because I never had much freedom, I wanted to put myself in a place where I could have it. Because I never had the help that I wanted growing up, I'm always the first one to help someone in need. Because I grew up without my father, I aspired to become a good father, not wanting my children to feel the effects of an absent dad. Because I was bullied at different stages of my life (whether at school, work, or in my neighborhoods), I chose to put myself in a position where I would never be someone's pushover—and, boy, did I!

All throughout my life, my negative experiences were awakening a giant in me—one that never settles for mediocrity or a simply average life. I've always challenged myself, taking advantage of gifts and opportunities presented to me. In doing so, the things in my life that were supposed to destroy me became the greatest tools in my creation. Mediocrity is so evident in our present day that, if one is not diligent and focused enough, it will definitely suck them into an endless pit of failures.

Though it is OK for some, we have also been trapped in a world that thinks average is OK. Worse than that, it *is* OK in our communities, families, work environments, and relationships, with every step toward success scorned and laughed at, rather than motivated, encouraged, and fully supported. In an environment like that, one must quickly develop principles and characteristics that will help them overcome these mountains of mediocre perceptions that have plagued them, their families, and friends for generations. At times, breaking the cycle or curse, only takes that one individual who is frustrated with the norm and decides to do something about it, despite the criticisms.

Note: There is seldom anything OK about living the norm; only a life that has been suffocated with the chains of mediocrity.

For one to realize their curse and step out of the pit of unknown greatness is one of the most important stepping stones of life. For the realization of purpose has enough power in it to break the strong chains of mediocrity. We are living in a world where the term "average" is dying. For as the rich get richer, the poor get poorer, and I'm not speaking only financially but internally as well. You really only have two choices: achieving the freedom to do all that you wish and fulfilling your dreams; or hoping someone will provide it for you—which we all know never happens (this world gives no handouts). There are people out there who will enslave you and put you in a place where you can never reach the level of success that they have, in order to affirm to themselves that they are better than you. Some are so intimidated by your gifts and talents that they become threatened by you. If those people are at a place where they can easily get rid of you, they will do so in a flash. It is a sad world that we are living in *when the downfall of one is the glory of another, or the success of one is paid for with the failure of another.* As such, no one should put themselves in a place where they have to depend on someone else to help them live a life of great importance. By doing so, they put themselves in a place of vulnerability.

Mediocrity in relationships

Relationship beginnings are very critical moments in one's life. Until that point, you've been making decisions on your own—decisions to go to school, wake up at a certain time, eat at certain times, express your daily habits (whether good or bad) without been questioned, watch your television show knowing that no one is going to change the station. Everything you are and what you are about, including your personality and personal perception of life, follow you wherever you go, especially into relationships.

If you have lived a life of mediocrity and are going into a relationship with someone, you are going into it with baggage that you've been carrying around, good or bad, and also having to deal with baggage from the other person. Counselors and mentors are always stressing the importance of being careful not to go into a relationship without knowing who your partner is.

The problem is that people now get into relationships based on how good they feel about the person after a couple of dates, their physical appearance, or because they feel like he or she is a good person. These relationships usually end up in turmoil or misunderstandings, because people never take the time to do a more thorough search regarding the person they want to spend their lifetime with. Most people are afraid to be single, so they choose to take their chances on someone they're not sure of, hoping that they might turn out OK. They even sleep with them, assuming that they will stay or treat them better if they do.

That is one of the greatest lies Hollywood and other sources of influence have taught you. It is a very dangerous place to be in. Some things were not meant to be rushed, *especially relationships.*

Note: The negativity of one can cripple the productivity of another.

Going into a relationship can be a good thing, but it can also be a stumbling block, if one of the individuals is lazy, lacks focus, is not passionate or goal-oriented, is fearful to take chances, is OK with the normal life, and always sees the negative in everything. If you have ended up with someone who possesses some or most of these qualities, then you have ended up with someone who is trapped in a very deep state of mediocrity. Every positive choice that one tries to make to get ahead will be scorned by their mediocrity and will keep the both of you stuck at the same place you started twenty years ago. You must then make a very difficult decision of whether to stay in that relationship, and hope the individual might change—the chances of which are slim to none—or get out of that relationship in order to persevere and become a better you in every area of your life.

Note: Relationships are simple; you should marry what is going to add to you and complement you and your goals, not what brings you down.

Some stagnant relationships, whether caused by one mediocre-thinking individual or two, easily make room for all forms of disasters, including frustration, quarrels, constant disagreements, adultery, hatred, and a lack of money, which in many cases will lead to divorce. People who are fulfilled in life are rarely involved in marital problems.

I've come to discover that, in most cases, it's not the money that makes these people happy, but the peace and abundant supply of strength from their well-established identity as a person. All these being sufficient, it is very hard for them to react to the deficiencies listed above. This is because they have developed positive life principles along their journey to becoming who they are, which in return followed them right into their relationships and other areas of their lives.

As for those whose relationships are just hanging by a thread, they failed to deal with some issues before they chose to be with someone else. Some marry into mediocrity and some are already trapped or satisfied there, so they only know how to search for themselves: another person with mediocrity. This then will easily pass on to their children, and sadly their children after them—a generational curse.

A simple mistake that most people make is that they get into relationships not taking the time to first know what they want in life, so that they may best know the kind of person they want to spend the rest of their lives with. Instead, they get into relationships because they are looking for someone to fill the wounded and empty places in their hearts, out of the fear of just being alone, or just looking for someone to caress them and be emotionally attached to. Hence, they make room for being wounded some more, rather than getting the healing they need by first going through the process of self-discovery. It is almost impossible for a human to be a healing source for another, for every individual has their own issues from which they are trying to be healed. While the goal-oriented person wants to achieve great things, set goals, fulfill their dreams, work toward their passions, and stir up their ambitions, the mediocre person is dealing with insecurities, low self-esteem, grudges, or jealousy toward another based on their past failures, pride, or even arrogance. It should be a no-brainer that you should not get into a relationship with someone like that. For the day you do, you are marrying into a situation that will pull you down for a very long time.

One must take a serious season in time to discover first who they are as a person, from weaknesses to strengths, bad habits to productive characteristics, and what they need to be in life, before they think about looking for someone to spend it with. For knowing who you are will help you choose the individual you really want to spend your time with. Focus on your dreams and the goals you've set to achieve them, and whoever is for you will meet you along that path while they are similarly pursuing life's best!

Note: One who perseveres to make their dreams come true is sure to meet someone like-minded along the way.

Mediocrity in the workplace

There are no such things as dead-end jobs, only dead-end thinking. For a positive employee, in any given work environment, there is room to grow. Now, there are some work environments in which everyone from the manager down to the supervisors is overflowing with pride, partiality, and hatred for those who choose not to cheat other companies, lie to clients, treat their employees unfairly, and even hide damaged products in between good ones before they are delivered so that their clients won't see them. I can personally attest to this. I've seen it all. These work environments can be very difficult to deal with, and one would rarely get a chance to grow as a person there. If you cannot change that system, because you're not in a position to do so, then you must seek counsel from government offices, labor boards, and private programs in order to take you through a step-by-step process for getting such problems fixed.

In other matters, whether you're working for a big corporation or a small business, it is very rare that you see someone with a positive attitude and a good work ethic remain at one position for long; their personality and purpose-driven state of mind will always make room for them to excel in any given environment. It is their nature to do their best, and it has been proven that, if someone works and gives their best at a particular workplace for at least ten years, they are most likely going to be playing a leading role at the top of the company because of their efforts. This is because, subconsciously, they always seek to improve their company, themselves, and their co-workers, and to give a helping hand to whomever needs it, whether requested or not. This type of commitment will definitely be noticed over time, and corporations and businesses will make room for such individuals in order for their company to grow. Owners, CEOs, presidents, and managers of great companies are easily drawn to people who are driven and have the work ethic to prove it. These are the type of people they will invite into their circle of influence, and open doors for them that they never thought were possible.

When mediocre people go into the workforce, their story is a little different. First and foremost, they are fine at any position you place them in, and the company won't mind it, as long as they are doing what they are supposed to. But they likely won't want to grow or do anything that indicates that they want to get ahead in the company or in life; they just do enough to get paid and keep the job. These types of people bring their issues outside of work into the workplace. Their negative personalities cause a chain reaction that, when not dealt with, can spread to the other employees. They go about initiating acts of gossip, division, arrogance, mischief, deceit, anger, frustration, jealousy, drugs, greed, and more. These characteristics are the fruits of having a mediocre mindset and embracing it. As I've mentioned before, though not all those in mediocrity are bent on spreading negative ideologies, there *are* those who prey on people who give them the ear to spread their negative thinking. Ultimately, being mediocre and not striving toward anything is not really the issue, because if you don't want to be the best you can be, that is fine. That's on you. What one should worry about is the fruits that are born of mediocrity, which will eventually hurt the individual and those around them.

Humans do not realize that, as we grow from childhood into adulthood, we develop terrible habits and personalities, whether they stem from traditions, systems, or protocols that we are accustomed to, neighborhoods that we live in, or even just an accumulation of past hurts and family issues. And we bring all these weights into the workplace. The good thing about those who set goals and strive toward them is that the journey will include some challenges and demands that require them to give up all the nasty principles, bad character traits, and terrible habits that they have picked up earlier in their lives, and this will cause them to make a positive change in their lives and personalities, and make them much better people to be around. It will also make them good leaders that others look to for guidance.

As for those who choose not to aspire to become anything or accept the challenges that come with the journey of changing their situation or personality for the better, choosing instead to remain in mediocrity, unmoved by anything, negatively sitting in one place, not having anything to do with productivity, and blaming everyone else for their failures, they will remain surrounded by all the negative fruits that mediocrity bears, disappearing behind them as they pile up, waiting for their greatest downfall and contaminating their surroundings and everyone in it.

Mediocrity in goal-setting

People who set goals in life, based on either things they would like to accomplish or simple things to help them grow as a person, are constantly busy, not making room for any idle moment. They are so consumed with where they want to be in life that distractions and negativity do not thrive in their midst. Sometimes, they even find it difficult to keep friends, and so are often alone. Their goals at times are so big that, even after they've accomplished a portion of them, they push even harder than before. They accept the process. Their focus on their destination makes them a force to be reckoned with. Goals are a part of every individual's life, whether it be to develop personally, finish school, graduate with excellence, have an amazing career, marriage, or family, or help their employers with their company.

The difference between people with ambition who set goals, and those of mediocrity who set goals, is that those who are ambitious about accomplishing something set their hearts to see it through, no matter how hard it is or how long it takes. The negative perceptions of those in mediocrity get in the way very early in their journey, and they give up at any sign of discomfort, internal and external.

The choices we make in our everyday lives will eventually lead us to the people we will become tomorrow. If they're bad choices, then we will reap the fruits thereof; if they're good choices, acted upon over time, they will surely lead to some form of success in the individual's life.

For success is only small positive decisions consistently made on a daily basis, added up over time, leading to something great.

The problem is that people set their goals and do not have the mental discipline to follow through, especially those with a mediocre mindset.

There are others living a life of mediocrity who do not bother setting major goals in their lives. If they are in the workforce, they wake up in the morning, go to work, go home, grab a beer, turn on the television, watch their favorite show or sports, then go to bed in preparation for work in the morning. If that's as far as your aspirations for your life goes, then all the best to you. At least you're working and taking care of yourself and possibly a family.

But for me and others, there is more to life than just being average. The idea of setting goals, for some people, is an atrocity and an insult. Most of these people are very well aware that they are stuck, but when one highlights their stagnancy or the state of their lives, their pride and anger come forth, making them defensive. And that's not because the other individual is wrong, but to hide their insecurities, failures, and the deficiencies of their current state. At some point in their lives, they must have tried accomplishing some goals but failed. It could have been because they are weak emotionally, not passionate enough, or didn't have the tenacity and the character required to carry on, as they witness others with the same goals pass right by them toward success. As a result, they become angry, frustrated at themselves, and jealous at those who made it.

What such people must understand is that fear, doubts, shortcomings, failures, and even a lack of qualifications are all a part of the process, for the journey will reveal everything in one's heart, both weaknesses and strengths. As such, you have got to see the difficulties, embrace them, accept the mistakes and shortcomings, and keep on persevering regardless, bringing about the positive process of change. That's the key! That's what separates failures from champions!

Note: Though the heart of a champion is recognized after they've been victorious in battle, it was molded in the fire of their past afflictions.

The goals of mediocre people don't go as far as anything that makes them feel uncomfortable. They will scorn the idea and adventure simply to hide and protect their deepest insecurities. They will take part in anything except that which challenges them to heal their hearts and change their perceptions of life. If they have a family of their own, they are not just a curse to themselves, but to their spouses, and even to their children.

Note: A man (human) is not a man until he has embraced and overcome the challenges that come to him in life, as he perseveres toward building character and becoming his ultimate best.

Mediocrity in ministry

Mediocrity in ministry is not too different from that of the world; it is only a different atmosphere. Mediocrity is not hard to pick up on; anywhere there is no productivity or growth, there is a good chance that some form of mediocrity is at play. How active a person is in their communities, country, and even (more importantly) world, will quickly reveal whether or not a ministry is striving to reach its fullest potential. We cannot judge any ministry based solely on our perception of what a fruitful ministry is. The best way to clearly judge whether or not a ministry is doing what it's supposed to do is to read the scriptures.

I will highlight a few verses to give us an idea of how some of these ministries should be.

Jesus made it clear, in John 10:10, *"I have come to give life, and that you might have it more abundantly"* (not some or little-abundantly). In John 13:34, Jesus told his disciples to *"love one another as he has loved them."* He also told them, in Matthew 5:44, to *"love their enemies, bless them that curse you, do good to them that hate you, and pray for them which despitefully use you and persecute you."*

I could quote an unending number of scriptures upon which Jesus taught his disciples many things of how ministry should be, telling them to teach others the same thing. He then went on to heal the blind, cleanse the lepers, and make the lame walk. To cause deaf ears to hear and manifest countless signs and wonders. Even long after he left, his disciples and those after them continue the ministry, impacting people's lives, feeding the poor, tending to widows, establishing more ministries worldwide, and changing neighborhoods, communities, and nations. Wherever they went to minister, hundreds of people would join them and become free from strongholds, depression, sickness, diseases, and all forms of oppression.

So what happened to most of the ministries nowadays? It's simple, really: They brought into the church their human nature and the same mediocre way of thinking that they have attained from their culture, workplaces, and neighborhoods throughout their lives. If they are stuck in their lives overall, and have not dealt with their mediocre state of mind, then they are most likely to be stuck wherever they go, including the ministry, from the pastor right on down to the least of their congregation. Mediocrity is not partial to status; it can enter the heart and mind of anyone.

I've been around different denominations and observed how every one of these ministries is unique in their own right. What I've noticed throughout the years is that the ones that are most fruitful are those who genuinely love people and are compassionate toward them. As a result, they are very active in their communities and societies. Some go as far as supporting many other ministries outside their own country, helping victims whose nations are at war or in poverty. This is amazing to see, and the thrill I get over such productivity in these ministries wows me, for I also feel a great sense of compassion.

I love people, and seeing their lives go from negative to positive is a high I get without the influence of any drugs. As for those who have been in ministry for over twenty years, with, let's say, 350 seats in their sanctuary, and still only have just fifty members, there is almost always a problem. One cannot judge quickly but rather observe, as I did, to find out what problem there might be that is keeping that ministry from being more fruitful after so long. So, why aren't they fruitful like the others? There are many reasons. They set goals and do not fulfill them. They make promises and do not keep them. They will say the right things behind the pulpit, because they have been trained to do so, and yet don't practice what they preach. They speak of love and yet gossip and criticize those who don't look or act like them. They condemn every denomination but their own. They speak highly of helping the poor and yet have not reached out to their own community. And if they have, they are not as consistent as they should be, doing it only based on conscience and guilt rather than love.

They can look very righteous on the outside, but their hearts are unclean, full of pride, deceptive, and mischievous—cunning tricks to keep people under their form of control. Their exterior is well-dressed, but their hearts are naked. These types of people are what I call "present-day Pharisees." In truth, God will not exalt a ministry of such, not because He hates them but because He refuses to elevate them in order to show them that they are doing something actively wrong that is hindering their blessings. The sad part is that, instead of correcting their perceptions and foolish ideologies of what ministry is, they invent their own righteousness in order to replace God's. They come up with systems, laws based on culture and traditions, man-made rules, and dress codes, and stubbornly affirm their own beliefs that this is how ministry should be done, despite their stagnant state. What they pass onto others will then be based on their commitment to do what they've been told and abide by the laws set by their leaders, present and past. Hence, they become humanly religious, like the Pharisees of old, instead of a genuine spiritual life with their God; serving God with their lips rather than their hearts.

Note: Religiosity in any faith is man's method of trying to imitate the righteousness of almighty God.

I had been in a ministry where there were just over 300 seats and seventy members, but only about forty people who consistently attended services. The ministry was more than twenty years old and for over seven years I observed and tried to play my part to build it. The pastor had many ideas, goals, dreams, and passions, which he always shared with the people, motivating them and establishing hope that it would all come to pass, and the ministry would be fruitful and even spread throughout the nation. But as I observed his state of mind combined with his actions and principles, I saw that his actions did not match the required efforts to fulfill and build his ministry; he would do everything right in regards to working at church tirelessly, and remain committed to it, but the systems, traditions, and man-made rules that he was accustomed to and believed to be the only way church was done, kept him and his ministry stuck. He knew the earthly church, not the Kingdom one, and there is a difference. Most people think that God is going to do everything for them, but God already did something. Outside of the sacrifice of the cross, we now know that in every human there are gifts and talents that are of much value. The problem is that most people bury them and expect God to bless them. What they don't realize is that God is waiting for you to present your gifts from within, so that He may do his part and stretch them throughout the nations, to bless you. And this, in return will bless others, and bring showers of blessings to everything around you. How can He elevate you when you've buried the same thing He created you to give life to? He came in flesh and paid the price to break the cursed chains of sin that had kept our true potential in prison. Now that you're free, what gifts or abilities are in you that you can exercise so that God can have something to work with in order to elevate and inspire others through you? It could be an album, a book, an idea, a vision or dream, a business, and much, much more. *But instead, most of us choose to live the average life of mediocrity, even though we have access to unlimited resources, especially in ministry.*

Mediocre folks have defined ministry based on the traditions, man-made rules, customs, systems, protocols, and even baptisms that they've been taught—the way of life that they, and those before them, have approved as righteousness. They are more focused on going to heaven, and live on earth just to get by. They live righteously to the best of their knowledge, just waiting in mediocrity for the rapture, as they say. But ministry is much more than that. Surely, we all want to go and rest for eternity. True. But our duty now, as we are in this human body, is to bring heaven down to earth. We've been given the authority, based on scripture, to do so, and yet mediocrity tells people that they should just hang in there, because Jesus is coming soon. Wrong. And so, even though God keeps them from harm or danger, He never elevates ministries with such thinking. He will not allow or permit them to represent Him on the world stage. Ministries that bring heaven down to earth touch those who are in poverty and need, the unfortunate ones in war-torn countries and bad neighborhoods, people inspiring their own nations. They go into government to make an impact and much more. Basically, wherever there is a problem, the ministries that are effective and are bearing fruit will go, changing nations for the better. As for those who are in mediocrity, just waiting for Jesus to come and liberate them from their misery, they remain stagnant and unfulfilled as God continues to work with those who are busy exercising their gifts and abilities in order to save more lives before His return.

The Pharisees were not mediocre financially, for they were busy acting righteous while secretly robbing the people of their money, and turning God's temple or ministry into a place of business and profit rather than a place of trust, hope, deliverance, and self-discovery for all. We have leaders in ministries nowadays that use their gatherings to gain personal profit and riches, as well, rather than having the people's interests at heart, but that's another topic for another time.

What Pharisees have in common with those of mediocrity today are the things they do to try and get approval from people, and for many different reasons. Just like the Pharisees of old; they do not practice what they teach. They bring about heavy burdens and put them on the shoulders of their followers, making them carry it, when they themselves are not willing to lift even a finger. They do all their "good work" specifically to be seen by people. They wear fine suits and beautiful dresses to look the part, and yet walk by the homeless every day and not bother to buy them food to eat. They love the place of honor at banquets and the best seats in their gatherings. They love elaborate greetings by all, and they love when people address them by the title minister, pastor, or bishop. The scriptures made it clear what these people, who know how to play the part and yet whose actions bear no fruit, are: hypocrites!

I have come to realize that there are better actors in church than in Hollywood. Their man-made rules, keep people on their benches, and deter them from becoming the best they can be. They are not just bearing no fruit; they also hinder or stop those of us who are trying to do so. They quote statements that have been passed on by those before to say to people like myself, who are ambitious and want more from life. They know what to say in order to hinder us, things like:

> "The love of money is the root of all evil."

> "It is hard for a rich man to enter the gates of heaven."

> "Naked I came into the world and naked will I leave."

"Follow and obey your elders, because God sent you to them, and he makes no mistakes."

"Humble yourself under the mighty hand of God, and he will exalt you in due time."

"The Lord giveth and the Lord taketh away."

Though all these statements sound nice, these mediocre folks are not using them because they know they are right, but to justify their stagnancy. To protect their insecurities and failures, they try to hinder those who are trying to get ahead, as they continue to keep making excuses for their ministries' failure to grow.

Sometimes, such people in the ministry will go through hell and high water to get people to attend their services, and when the people do, they leave feeling much worse than when they went in. Perhaps it's how they dress, or maybe their appearance. Perhaps they are scorned for not going to the altar when asked to, which leads to them feeling isolated, different, and many more foolish things. Whatever the issue might be, it makes the return of their newcomer very unlikely.

Those of mediocrity will then make excuses: *"This church thing is not for everyone."* Well, that is a lie. The church thing is for everyone. *It is their customs, systems, and foolish traditions, which they call righteousness, that is not for everyone.* It is their cursed mediocre state of mind that has brought all the mess and foolish man-made protocols into God's church, and made it difficult for poor souls to receive their breakthrough. If they do stay, which is very rare, the newly converted individual becomes mediocre in the same manner as the people with whom they are now associating themselves, innocently adapting to what is being taught, perceiving it to be the truth. They clean the outside of the dish, but inside, they are full of the same mediocre way of thinking that they walked in with, and self-indulgence. The blind leading the blind.

They should first clean the inside of the cup, so that the outside may become clean, also. The truth is that many of the people in these ministries, with a mediocre state of mind, are not whole at all, but empty, so they land some type of position in the ministry that makes them feel some level of importance, when all the while they are really longing to fill the void of their insecurities, failures, and shortcomings in life.

Other ministries in mediocrity applied some form of witchcraft system to keep people bound under their control, rather than giving them the freedom that God grants to all men to exercise their gifts and put them in surroundings where they can excel in life, reaping the fullness of their joy. According to those in a position of authority in some of these mediocre ministries, God has given them control over their followers, along with control over the choices they make. when attending these ministries, these are the signs that an individual must look for that indicate that these types of leaders are not really representing God as they proclaim to be:

> *The leadership will teach that God must speak to them first before He speaks to the individual.*
>
> *The leadership will curse any that leave their ministry.*
>
> *They will teach that their denomination is the only truth.*
>
> *They will forbid or prevent their members from talking to anyone who has left their ministry.*
>
> *They over-emphasize that one must be submissive to leadership.*
>
> *The leadership forbade their followers from visiting any ministry that is outside their denomination.*

Their sermons are sometimes made to hit and demoralized people from the pulpit, if they sense you're not going with everything they say.

People are afraid to voice any opinion to the leadership.

Marriages are sometimes broken by leadership.

People are manipulated regarding their giving.

Every decision that an individual makes in their personal life has to be approved by leadership.

People are forbidden from having fellowship with members of their family, if they are not saved and not part of their ministry.

People are discouraged from reading books that are not approved by leadership.

These types of leaderships are a curse to themselves and the people who follow them. Their form of mediocrity keeps people stuck in one place beneath their leadership. They use their power and various forms of control to keep people subjected to their perception of what ministry is, and yet are not going anywhere and so neither are those who follow them. In a few cases, people among them who want to achieve more in life escape these types of environments, and search for something or some other ministry that is more purpose-driven, rather than staying with those who are comfortable being in the swamp of mediocrity.

I believe that we are in the era when God is going to utterly shut down ministries of such mediocre thinking, and send His beloved people to other ministries that will help them grow in their gifts and abilities, and expand their horizons in order for His kingdom to go forth throughout the nations before His return, so that His people will fulfill their life's purpose.

CHAPTER 7
THE TRANSITION

Note: Our human nature has the tendency to persevere until it comes face to face with the discomfort of change.

Many of us don't mind going after what we want, from fulfilling our greatest dreams to being in a place of contentment. We persevere and strive in all that we do. The hopes of getting to our destination and staying there can sometimes overwhelm us with joy—which, in turn, motivates and empowers us to keep moving forward. We look forward to changing our lives and the lives of our loved ones, building businesses, establishing life-changing ministries, changing our communities, and reaching out to nations as we exercise our gifts in order to bless the hearts and souls of many. So what happens along the way, since only a very small minority get their breakthrough, and the majority quit? Discomfort.

It is because of the discomfort of change, inherent in the transition from what we've been accustomed to and where we are trying to go. The transition brings about a change of environment and a different system from what we know. This transition leads us to the unknown—an unknown territory, not necessary in terms of a physical location, but in terms of its demand for a new attitude, way of thinking, way of talking, way of discipline and responsibility. This will be a different system than the one you started with, a different playground that will cause you to leave behind your old ways of doing things and adapt to new ones. Transition is the stage that every successful individual has to go through at some point in their journey. The clash, coming face to face with this giant of change, can be incredibly uncomfortable for most people, not because it is a bad thing but because it stirs up something in them that they would rather keep in the shadows. The discomfort begins to consume the individual. It reveals weaknesses, and stirs up doubt, pride, low self-esteem, and fear, and generally causes a great level of frustration as the individual begins to realize that, in the unknown territory, the control they've had from the beginning over their emotions, decisions, ideas, methods, and so on, is quietly slipping away. This sends a great panic through the individual, and they throw in the towel, because they did not understand what to do in that place of transition.

As children, any new learning about the human soul can cause some level of discomfort. And as we grow, we experience change all the time, most of which includes some level of discomfort. And yet we do not realize it because it seems common to us. From breastfeeding to using baby bottles, drinking liquids to eating solid foods, crawling to standing and then walking, kindergarten through elementary, high school, college and the workforce and our own homes. All of these are transitions that we've experienced in our lives.

Though they were not comfortable at the time, our human will tends to adapt to any environment we're placed in and any situation we're faced with. Despite the change and discomfort of the unknown, we adjust and keep on moving.

We must come to the understanding that, as long as we keep striving toward our purpose, changes are constant events that will keep on occurring in our lives. They just take a different shape every time we get closer to our destiny—from basic changes to drastic ones. So, we might as well get used to them. The reason some people give up on the transition from all that they know to the unknown is that the change they're facing is unlike any other in the journey of their lives. It is the change that could catapult us to our destiny, and so it demands an internal adjustment in our emotions and habits.

This process in this stage of one's life is very much necessary. One's old state of mind and old way of thinking cannot survive in the vicinity of destiny. So the transition is merely there to prepare us for what is to come. Those who want it badly enough will endure through the uncomfortable territory and embrace the change it brings, while those who fear and choke on these changes will stay back and remain in mediocrity.

The level of discomfort in the transition of change from past understandings to developing new traits, methods, creativity, innovation, emotions, and more, can cause a great deal of confusion and turmoil in the hearts of people at this stage in their lives. This is why we came up with the saying *"only the strong survive."* Many people do not understand that the strength needed to be all we can be in life is far more than just making yourself available or using physical strength. It calls for mental toughness and emotional flexibility to adjust to the new environment presented to us.

I watched a documentary on the life of sea turtles, from eggs to their adulthood. The eggs hatch and the baby sea turtles must find their way to the water for many reasons. If they remain on land, they might die of starvation, overheating from the sun, becoming prey to predators or getting buried by the same sand on which their eggs were hatched.

Watching a baby sea turtle, known as a hatchling, struggle out of the nest and make its way to the water is an emotional experience. Everything from footprints to driftwood and crabs are obstacles to this challenge critical to its survival. Birds, raccoons, and fish are just a few of the predators these vulnerable creatures face. Some experts say that only one out of a thousand will survive to adulthood under natural conditions. After an adult female sea turtle nests, she returns to the sea, leaving her nests and the eggs within it to develop on their own. The amount of time the eggs take to hatch varies among the different species, and is influenced by environmental conditions such as the temperature of the sand. Once out of their eggs, they will remain in the nest for a number of days. During this time, they will absorb their yolk, which is attached by the umbilical cord to their abdomen. This yolk will provide them the much-needed energy for their first few days, as they try to make their way from the nest to offshore waters. It's interesting to note that, as the hatchlings begin to climb out the nest in a coordinated effort, once near the surface, they will often remain there until the temperature of the sand cools—usually nighttime—when they are less likely to be eaten by predators or get burnt by the sun. After that, they use cues to find the water, including the slope of the beach, the white crest of the waves, and the natural light of the ocean horizon. If the hatchlings successfully make it down the beach and reach the water, they begin what is called a "swimming frenzy," which may last for several days, and varies in intensity and duration among species. This frenzy gets the hatchlings away from dangerous near-shore waters, where predation is high. Once hatchlings enter the water, their "lost years" begin, and their whereabouts will be unknown (to human observers) for as long as a decade. Then, when they have reached the approximate size of a dinner plate, the young turtles will return to coastal areas, where they will forage and continue to mature.

When observed carefully, the sea turtle's experience and our human journey are very similar. As we've read, they remain in their nests for a few days, then eat the yolk connected to their abdomen. There is a season in our lives when we are in the nests of our parents, or any form of security, and have to learn or "eat" all we can (in terms of knowledge) in order to prepare us for the journey of life. Just as the turtle cannot stay in the nest where it was hatched because of the dangers around it, adults cannot stay wrapped in the security of those who have sheltered us from the time of our childhood, for if we do not step out and take the initiative to look for the ocean, we rob ourselves of the chance to embrace those challenges ahead that will bring out the best in us.

In some cases, some of us do stay with our parents or guardians, of course, working with them to accomplish a family goal, but this does not mean there won't be any kind of development experiences ahead that will shape or destroy them. Some of the larger sea turtles have a better chance of surviving the dangers and challenges that come with the journey. As humans, the journey of our lives brings about all forms of danger in the unknown, not to mention the different circumstances or "temperatures" that life brings. It takes an individual with a "larger" human will to survive it all.

Another unique event in the experience of these sea turtles is that, as a guide, they need the natural light of the ocean to lead them to the right place. Any other lights—such as from beach lights, street lights, cars, campfires, and so on—can lead them astray. Many of us get distracted from our journey by the simplest things. We lift our attention off it as things get difficult, and take detours to make ourselves feel better. People present to us another light, different from that which we were chasing, but it is a counterfeit light, the kind that can come from intimate relationships, friends, parties, jobs, and so forth, that comes only to lure us away from the journey before us.

Out of the nests, the sea turtles face many dangers, such as ghost crabs, birds, raccoons, dogs, and eventually fish. But the sea turtle *needs* the predators, because they give it the will and motivation to try its best to make it to the ocean. Our afflictions, emotional swings, obstacles and so on should do nothing more than motivate us even more strongly to get to our destination, lest we be eaten or swallowed up by the pressures of life.

I mentioned that when the sea turtle is still an egg, it needs the right environmental conditions in order for it to be hatched. Sometimes, it takes the most difficult situations, challenges, and changing conditions in our lives to actually help birth the purpose that is hidden deep within us. To climb out of the nests, the sea turtles use a coordinated strategy to get out. The truth is, as humans, there are times we must be able to discern when we need the combined help of others who share the same goals to get to where we want to be.

When in the ocean, the "swimming frenzy" stage of the sea turtle helps it get away from danger, at the cost of nonstop activity, for if it misses the right current, it will be pushed back to shore and dangerous predators. As humans, after we've touched and discovered the environment in which we are the most effective, and when the destiny that we seek is in our reach, this is the time we must swim even harder and faster, flowing with the current that is pushing us closer to our destiny, rather than away from it.

When in the ocean, the sea turtle could be isolated for decades. We humans, too, can be isolated from all we know and love for a period, when discovering our purpose and trying to fulfill our destiny. The sea turtle, after being in the ocean for a long time while it grows into adulthood, comes back to the shore to continue its evolution into maturity. As humans, when we have attained what we had set out to become, let us not forget where we came from, for what we've learned in the ocean pursuing our goals can be a life testimony to those still on the sand.

Note: Never ignore past failures, for in them lies the secret of trying new things rather than repeating what never worked.

Most people make the mistake of stopping in the transition of change, because what they have proven to work in the past is not working anymore. As they fail multiple times, they tend to throw in the towel. *Failure, ladies and gentlemen, is no more than the cue that lets us know that this is just one more way that doesn't work. As such, we should keep trying till we find the one that does.*

People misinterpret failure, but it is one of the greatest tools for letting us know that we are a step closer to where we need to be. Our past failures are some of the best ingredients for stepping into our destiny. No one wants to remain in the past forever, which forces us to challenge our minds to think and be creative. It's only right for us to know what doesn't work by failing, so we can keep trying to discover what does. Most people look at themselves after they fail and assume they are stupid, not good enough, will never achieve anything, or should had become this person or that person. Or they wish their lives were like that "other" person, blaming themselves for every ounce of failure.

We must realize that *failure is an external incident, not an internal one.* Failure occurs in one's journey in order to stir up our internal genius, motivating it to find the answers. It does not happen so that we can condemn ourselves. That is what we are doing when we ignore our internal genius and allow failure to label us stupid or useless. Failures, when perceived as something negative, can bring about frustration and mental collapse, but when looked at as something positive, can change the life of the individual. For every time we fail in something, it builds character, knowledge, patience, mental toughness, perseverance, and courage. Every past failure in one's life is only going to bring about future successes.

Note: We are the company we keep; no man can be anything more than the associations they choose to embrace.

As children growing up, the influences we have are not nearly as important as the ones we have as adults. For as children, our only influences are introduced to us by our parents, guardians, counselors, etc. Some of these environments are expected, and we have little choice in any case. So when in these surroundings, as teenagers and as young adults, one must be very focused and cautious in all that they do. In school environments, we are introduced to different types of influences. We must make sure we choose the right ones or nothing at all. When we get older, things become a bit different. The influences we choose to be a part of are solely based on the understanding of who we are and who we see ourselves becoming. As adults, it is very vital to understand what we want out of life in order to make the right decisions. In doing so, we can best choose our own environment and the influences with which we want to associate . People (like children) who don't know what they want in life, or where they want to be, just end up with whatever influences life throws at them. If they're fortunate enough, they could end up with good influences that can help them discover their path in life and lead them to be all they can be. Sadly, this is not always the case, which is why the world is in the shape it's in as we speak.

As adults, it is best to know what we want from life and who we would like to become so we can choose the influences that will complement our goals and dreams. If you want to start a business, I suggest you hang out with people who have started businesses and have been successful with them. If you want to start some type of ministry or foundation, it's best you associate with people who have been successful with things of that nature. Regardless of what you want to pursue, take counsel from those people who will challenge, encourage, and support you as you chase after life's best, even if it doesn't always make sense to them.

Some people, though they have great aspirations, goals, and dreams, and even take steps to fulfill them, make the mistake of thinking that their associations do not affect their decisions or actions. That is as foolish as saying, "*If you throw a raw egg in a hot frying pan, it won't get fried.*" No matter how much tenacity you possess, no matter how many plans you've made, and no matter how strongly you've made up your mind to be successful, if you associate with people who do not want to go anywhere; don't want to become anything; lack the will to strive for anything; are lazy, negative, or satisfied with the norm, they will surely hinder, choke, or suffocate every ounce of positivity left in you just by being around them, if they don't try to stop you with their words.

There is another old saying: "*When you lie down with dogs, you'll stand up with fleas.*" In most cases, the negative influences or surroundings of mediocre people are hard to pick up on right away, but subconsciously, as time goes by, they gradually saturate us until we are totally consumed by what they believe. All of a sudden, things begin to change, and not for the better. You used to debate with them from dusk till dawn about not settling as they have, but now you don't mind hearing their opinions about your ambitious mentality. You used to wake up early to spend time meditating on your dreams and goals, but now you're just waking up to go to work like everyone else. You used to go to seminars and business-development meetings, but now you're fine with just hanging out with the boys at the bar. You used to save up every penny you could for future investments on things pertaining to the goals you'd set, but now you're always going to the mall and spending money on clothing with your friends. What happened? Your negative influences have found a way to slowly attach their way of thinking to your spirit, and are beginning to suffocate the energy and life source of all that drives you. When purpose is conceived, and the will to become successful in life is embraced, we must then take the initiative to associate ourselves with people who are like-minded or have already done what we are trying to accomplish with integrity and character.

As we begin to change our environments of negative influences, we must not forget that, in the transition of change, the most important change of all is transforming the mindset we once had into one that complements our future aspirations. This is key to your journey. For no matter how much effort you've put into changing your environment, influences, neighborhoods, associations, and so on, if you don't change your mindset, all your sacrifices are for nothing. This is the most important factor in the transition of change.

Note: Picture the human mind like tea in a cup; how sweet it gets depends on how much sugar you put in it.

Note: The human mind is like a child; it can only process what you introduce it to.

No man can become any more than what their minds have conceived. If the mind belongs to an individual who doesn't want to learn anything or be anything, then that's what their minds will process; if the mind belongs to one who is an addict or an alcoholic, then it will assume that it is OK to smoke and drink, even to the point of making excuses for their addiction in order to justify themselves. The mind will eventually tell itself that anything you've introduced to it is OK, because you've trained it to think like that, even if that state is not naturally good for you, physically or mentally.

So, the place of mediocrity is only right to you because you've trained your mind to think it is. It's not OK for your family, it's not OK for your finances, and it's not OK for your life. But if the mind belongs to one who is constantly learning and has the will to persevere in life, then it won't just absorb all that the individual is learning but will also be able to come up with ideas and creativity supernaturally, in order to help that individual achieve their goals.

Note: The key of change is a mind made up and the human will that drives it.

Everything after that is just consistency—doing daily what you've proven works for you in order to get ahead in your life. Falling into a mindset of mediocrity is much easier than trying to get out of it. *"If you raise a child to believe a lie, when they grow up, they will take the truth to be false."* This is sad but true. Throughout our lives, we've taken in so much garbage from a world full of small thinking and waywardness that the time of transitioning into a better version can be very challenging. It is as though we have to become children all over again, taking baby steps to educate ourselves—but this time for the purpose of who we see ourselves becoming tomorrow, by learning from people who have done it, educating our minds, choosing a better circle of friends, and so on. All this can be very difficult to do when you're trying to flush a mindset of mediocrity and develop one that's purpose-driven. But it's important and must be done consistently and with focus in order to break from this cursed state of a mediocre mind. When we see people in mediocrity who are OK with it, this just means that their minds have not been trained to think anywhere outside their current state in life, leaving them average and satisfied with just living in the norm.

I would also like to bring up a point about some of the habits that we must apply and some of the ones that we must forsake as we go through the transition of change. We occupy ourselves with so many things that are of no importance to us. What we should really be spending our time on is the kind of legacy we will leave behind for our loved ones, friends, societies, and nations of the world, since after we are buried, nothing will matter but that by which we are remembered.

We are so worried about things that are of little importance. We have become so used to indulging in activities and programs that we actually think the world will end without them. They *must* get done! For example, what is more important: never missing your child's baseball game or leaving a legacy that they can inherit from you? What is more important: the car you drive and the house you live in or the wisdom you leave behind for people so that they, too, may live a life as fulfilled as yours? What is more important: all the parties you've been going to or the seminars you've attended by people with great knowledge and success? What is more important: how many hours you spent sleeping or what you did with your time while you were awake? All these questions will come to us on our deathbeds, as they have for many others before us, great and small, and it would be sad to realize that your life's actions were no more than a waste to a world in need of people living with purpose.

The world we're living in has more distractions than we can possibly think of. So in order for us to change our lives and transition, we must counter every distraction and bad habit we've grown accustomed to with something that will benefit us tomorrow, whether it be minor or epic. The amount of time we spend watching television should be cut off or shortened, and replaced with reading books or listening to motivational tapes that will stimulate our minds. The amount of time we spend in clubs, parties, drinking, campfires, gatherings, and fine banquets should be spent educating ourselves in some manner. The amount of time we spend having fun with our friends should be shortened, and replaced with going to seminars and personal-development meetings. As minor as some of these distractions might seem, when engaged in consistently over time, the life of the individual will be less fruitful than it should be. Alternatively, when one begins to change these bad habits and spend more time building good habits, that will benefit the individual in the future, the fruits of their labor will start to show, whether internally or externally. For when we are placed six feet under, we are not going to take anything with us—not our homes, not our cars, not our money, and not our belongings. We are going to leave everything behind us, seen or unseen.

So then, I say to us all, if we are going to leave everything behind anyway, why not leave behind a good reputation, a book, an album, an invention, a business, a ministry, a foundation, a community program, an inspirational life lived, overall? Why not leave behind an amazing legacy, so that on the day of your burial, or when somebody walks by your tombstone, people will say, "There once lived an individual who lived a life so fruitful that, even after their death, they still live among us, for their life's work is still with us today."

I've seen and heard of wars both past and present, none of them pretty. Innocent people are mostly the victims of such man-made conflicts. Whether the wars are fought between good against evil, for land or for money, or for just greed and a thirst for power, innocent people (mostly women and children) are usually the ones who are affected the most. Consider the two World Wars, the Korean War, the war against terrorism, the civil wars across the African continent, and ask yourself this question: When is this ever going to end? I don't know, but believe that it will. And as a Christian and a man of faith, I believe that redemption will come to those who endure to the end. I realize this might seem off topic, but I'd not highlight such atrocities if it didn't help illustrate the next points about transition that I'm going to make. What I want you, the reader, to realize and understand is that whether you have made up your mind to chase after your dreams or you're already chasing them, there is also a war that is going to take place in your mind—the war between your past system of doing things and the new system you're trying to adopt in order to get out of an average life. The old system versus the new system is the war within you, and you need to be mentally strong long enough to give the new system time to integrate itself into your way of thinking. You must first realize that your emotions, old habits, past standards you've lived by and morals you've followed, and even the belief system that you've embraced are all alive, and they only have one place to reside: in you. At the point when you're trying to end the relationship, they are going to put up a good and a painful fight, which at times can even give you a headache. They will remind you of how comfortable life was, how simple it was, how much time you had to yourself, how consistent the welfare checks were, what a steady job you had, how pleasurable life was, sitting in front of your flat-screen TV watching your sports with a cold beer in your hand. These past attributes that were engraved within you will do anything in their power to remain where they are, and refuse to be replaced by another system. These past systems will keep one in poverty, homelessness, wanting, lack, under the radar, unsatisfied, unfulfilled, lazy, and full of resentment, hate, anger, and even just hopelessness.

The key that one must acknowledge about those negative past systems is that they *know* they will eventually destroy your future somehow, so they try to hide inside of you by keeping you busy with unnecessary things and mindless distractions so they have enough time to take you to a place from which there is no return. Now, if your past system is working well for you, and getting you closer to your life's goals, then these comments obviously do not apply to you.

At the place of self-realization when the will to become something more kicks in, little by little, portions of the new system will start to integrate, and the fight of the inner-man will begin. The new system will bring about a new way of thinking, a new way of life, a new belief system, new standards, new morals, and new attributes that can bring about love, hope, perseverance, consistency, forgiveness, financial freedom, fulfillment, satisfaction, good relationships, and more. This is the clash of the Titans all over again. One system is there to keep you in bondage; the other comes in to awaken the champion in you, in order to set yourself free, and in return, set others free, as well.

How do you determine which system is going to win this war? It depends on the one you feed the most! You can either allow the old system to keep controlling your life, keeping you in a place as stagnant as a swamp, or you can allow the new system to integrate within your life and take over the old, letting you walk into a glorious future. It's not going to be easy, nor is it going to happen right away, but when you consistently feed the new system and forsake the old, you'll no doubt begin to reap the fruits thereof.

To defeat this old system is to fight and replace every old habit and way of thinking with something new. Counteracting a bad habit with a good one is one of the steps you should apply to defeat the old system. If you're reckless and lazy, then begin to take responsibility and develop a good work ethic. The system that is going to win this inner battle is the one you feed the most.

In the transition of change, people make the mistake of just doing it based on their personal knowledge or understanding. This can be very dangerous in an individual's journey, for there comes a time in everyone's life when they have to depend on their faith to pull them through. The mistake we humans make is that we only keep going forward because we see where we are going.

Note: Faith is persevering, even though the future looks uncertain.

One of the my best memories from my journey was the fact that, despite how many times I felt short, rejected, unqualified, not good enough, not looking the part, scorned and embarrassed, falsely accused, or failed, one thing was for sure: I was going to keep on moving, no matter how dark the future looked from where I was standing.

I have faith enough to know that, if I keep on going, maybe I will find a tree in this dry, hot desert of my life and get some shade. Nobody should be responsible for your failures but you. For if you quit because of somebody else's opinion of you and where you're going, you're a fool! No one has what it takes to stop the human will, not with their remarks, opinions, or comments. And not your boss, family, friends, or enemies. No power of any sort can stop you. The only person who can stop you *is you!*

My faith is the anchor of my successes, both small and great. Two things played a major role in my life: the human will that pushes me and the faith that carries me. I have seen many things in my life, some too much to bring up, but one thing I know is that life has many treacherous roads in it. Life is full of difficulties, misfortunes, failures, struggles, and hills and mountains to climb. Without faith, it is impossible for any man to make it past the mountains of life. It is not for us to know what is going to be beyond those mountains. We would love to know everything about the amazing future we're fighting so hard to achieve, but we can't. All we are responsible for is persevering and holding onto the faith that there is joy on the other side of the mountain, whether we can see it or not. There will be moments in our journey when we have tried everything we know to do, and yet come up short. The key here is not to quit on everything you've worked so hard on, but to keep doing what's required to stay in the fight with transition. Hang in there until that dark season is over. That, my friends, is faith at its best.

The transition of change demands much from us, but the end result makes it worth it all. It is true that the process of change carries much weight and can make the individual very weary. There is a strong physical demand required in this stage of your journey, the likes of which you've never encountered before. Your sleeping schedule might change. Your eating habits will change. The transition might require you to do more than you had intended, and your life will be boring, for you will be solely focused on what you're trying to do. This will often cause your body to be weak. *This is normal.* Do not think for a second that this is not supposed to happen. These necessary steps of physical sacrifice are totally expected in a place of transition. Another higher demand in this stage—in my case, a higher demand than the other—is mental. You must give great thought and mental energy to every decision and action you take. The mind can contain a lot, but when you're in a brand-new place in your life, it takes some time for it to adjust to new surroundings. Such a shakeup can mentally overwhelm you in a way that's much worse than being physically tired. At least if you're physically tired, you can get strength from your mental toughness and keep on going a little bit longer, but when you're mentally tired, your whole body shuts down, because when the mind is done, everything is done! With all this being said, we must make sure that we try our best not to repeat past mistakes. The human being is not perfect. That's why, time after time, we repeat the mistakes of our past, and get slowed down from reaching an expected end. Knowing that every effort, action, and step we take toward our goals is going to draw strength from both our bodies and minds, we must minimize mistakes as much as possible. Only by doing this can we reserve physical and mental strength for other challenges that will come our way. Often, in the transition of change, people assume that everything they've left behind is done for, and since they are on the verge of a breakthrough, they let loose and let their guards down. I call this "the comeback of old curses." At a place of breakthrough or success, things we used to do or people we used to be with (I call these "past demons") will always be right behind, waiting for you to slip. These past demons could be anything that was hindering you from getting ahead in life. It could be addiction (of any sort), negative family members, terrible past relationships, negative friends, and even distractions of any kind. Whether these past demons are people or just bad habits, you may have left them behind. But it doesn't mean they have stopped chasing after you. Your state of mind just began to move much faster than what they could keep up with.

In a sense, I look at it like being on a race track. The ambitious, hungry, and goal-oriented racers are always ahead of the small-timers and mediocre thinkers, but it doesn't mean that they are not behind them. The moment the ambitious racers slow down is when stragglers begin to catch up. The small-timers and mediocre racers are not going to simply fill up and share the space with the go-getters. They are also going to slow them down and hinder their progress toward the finish line. Knowing this, whether we are in the transition of change or have passed it and are now reaping some of the benefits we've worked so hard for, we can never stop. We must keep on going, adding knowledge, wisdom, happiness, fulfillment, and, of course, financial freedom in the new way of life we've embraced.

In the transition of change, I must stress a point that I mentioned only briefly earlier: People back down *in fear* of the moment they encounter a challenge they don't see themselves winning. It could be a situation, a decision, a boss, or any number of things. *But one must know that, without "fear," there would be no "courage."* I should carefully say then, that fear is a good thing, not because of what it brings, but because of what it stirs up within us: *courage*. We have to understand that the unknown future has a way of bringing us to places or situations that invite fear into our hearts. We have to develop a state of mind that lets us keep going, even though we feel the fear. *This is courage at its best!*

The transition of change from mediocrity to prosperity is also similar to the transition of change of a caterpillar to a butterfly. The prosperity I'm speaking of is not just that of finances but also richness in health, relationships, personality, and every other area of your life.

A man once told me a story. It was about an old man and a caterpillar he saw in his backyard. The story was sad, but very informative, and I think it best fits the point I'm trying to make right now:

> One day, an old man sat down in his backyard. After sitting there for some time, he saw a caterpillar travailing in its chrysalis, transforming into a butterfly. The old man saw that the caterpillar was struggling in its transforming stage, and, feeling pity for it, decided to assist. He reached out his hands and began to help the caterpillar come out of its chrysalis. After a brief moment, he was able to free the caterpillar, but what was supposed to be a moment of rejoicing became a moment of sadness, for after he had helped the caterpillar, it quickly died. What happened? If humans could understand what the old man realized at that point they would be encouraged to endure more in life than they do. The old man realized that the caterpillar needed to go through the struggle in its transforming stages. What he had thought bad for it was actually necessary in order for the caterpillar to complete its transformation into a butterfly. Through this transformation, two things happen to the caterpillar: some parts transform, some parts disappear completely. Every turn, pain, twist, struggle, and stretch

that the caterpillar had to endure was needed, because *"its current affliction was only the doorway into its fullest potential."* Sadly, the old man regretted his decision to interfere in the caterpillar's moment of triumph. He realized that he hadn't just destroyed the caterpillar's destiny; he had killed the purpose the caterpillar was supposed to fulfill.

What did we learn here? Much can be extracted from this story, but, briefly, the point of transition is neither pretty nor enjoyable. But like the caterpillar's transition, all the struggles and afflictions that occur in our own lives happen only to bring out the best in us. If it fails or is avoided, we are no more than a dead caterpillar in our chrysalis (box).

I can't help but think of what that caterpillar would have looked like as a butterfly. What color would its wings have been? What garden was it supposed to illuminate? What part in the circle of life was it supposed to play? The truth is that we will never know, for it was killed in the process of transition. This is very similar to us as humans. How can we receive or know the benefits of our greatest potential when we quit in the middle of our transition and prematurely abandon the journey that's leading us to becoming our greatest self?

> *"What the caterpillar calls the end of the world, the master calls a butterfly."*
>
> ~ *Richard D. Bach*

CHAPTER 8
A TASTE OF DESTINY

Note: The dreams of a man are so strong that, when acted upon, what was once a dream can become their reality.

It is hard in this dark world to picture something that we cannot see, especially what we would like to become. But life has a way of sometimes helping us get a taste of our destiny. If we don't see it externally, there is always something bubbling up within us, a subtle feeling accompanied by a sense of peace that helps us to imagine what the other side feels like. Have you ever imagined what life would be like when you're financially free and well-established, with your family in order, with friends who admire the fruits of your labor, with your gifts being exercised, your hopes reachable, your life being fulfilled, your mind free from oppression, your heart light (removed from the heaviness of previous life and changing the lives of others, inspiring nations), your testimony an example to many, and just about everything you do being blessed, even if it seems foolish? Though life feels like it's robbing us sometimes, it can also present to us things that can help us dream again, persevere, hope, and endure until those dreams come to fruition.

On a sunny day in spring some time ago, I was sitting down at a park enjoying myself. I was surrounded by nature: trees, grass, gardens, and the animals that resided there. Soon, a man walked by and happened to stop just about fifteen feet from where I was sitting to ask me a question.

"Have you ever wondered what it would feel like to be a tree, or the grass, a flower, or even one of those fluffy rabbits?"

I thought the question was silly, but because I am one who loves nature very much, could not help but join him in discussion. "No," I said, "I never really thought about it. Why would you ask a question like that?"

"Well," he said, "they don't have to worry about anything. No bills, no issues, no struggles, no pain, no taxes, and no pressure from friends or family. Nothing at all."

The man seemed very serious and genuine, so I quietly allowed myself to ponder for a few seconds. "So, you would like to be one of these creatures or a tree, huh?" I asked, finally.

"Yes," he said. "Gladly."

"Who is more important," I asked him, "the caretaker or what he is taking care of?" The man didn't answer so I continued. "That which is being taken care of has no more value than its source." The man was listening thoughtfully, and seemed ready to hear what I would say next.

"The trees, the animals, the beautiful gardens that we see, and all the wonderful things and views that nature provides, they were not created to take care of the human race, but rather the human race was created to take care of all that their eyes could see."

The man looked at me in awe. "I'm listening," he said eagerly. I nodded. "There are two points I would like to make clear to you, friend. No, they do not have to endure the things that we do, but that doesn't mean they are not having it rough, just as we are, for they have to live in the same world we are, where it is the survival of the fittest. Some have to draw from the soil for nutrients, and feed from the sun, and some have to hunt, and even store their foods to last them throughout the winter. Like these animals we're surrounded by, for instance," I said, looking at the squirrels and rabbits in the tall grass and the crows overhead.

"The next point I would like to make," I said to the man, "is that, though nature is a beautiful thing, the only reason we might like to 'be them,' as you've said, is if we, who are their supposed caretakers, have not realized the treasures within us. If you were created to tend to such beautiful wonders in nature, shouldn't there be something even more beautiful within *you?* To be able to know, recognize, and tend to what's beautiful outside of you?"

The man was stunned! He grabbed a seat and said to me, "No one has ever said something like that to me before."

"It is normal in our society nowadays to just think of ourselves as average," I replied. "But I assure you, friend, that we are not average. Our natural eyes and society have just blinded us to who we were truly created to be, and the amazing destiny that each one of us possesses and ought to fulfill."

In disbelief of what he had heard, the man looked for a long time at the beautiful natural scene in front of us, then said, "A few moments ago, I wanted to be like them, to get away from being me, when in truth . . . I wanted to find myself. Their survival *depends* on how much knowledge I have of *myself.*"

The man looked at me with a genuine smile, shook my hand firmly, and thanked me. I knew, in that moment, that that man's state was much different when he left than when he arrived. He'd just gotten a taste of his own destiny.

Every time there is an impulse to settle for what has been, revealed to us by our difficult circumstances, bad situations, and even things that seem impossible, there is always something within us that (if we're quiet enough) we can hear say, "You are worth something of great value. What you imagine can be real." Sadly, we have been taught by society that this is just wishful thinking. The poison of this thought has been a curse to us for generations.

There is no such thing as "wishful thinking" for the human race. Our design, our divine nature, is to imagine what we cannot see, and to bring it to life using our creativity and faith. This is the essence of the human race, friends. "We are born to call things that are not as though they were," for though we are created beings, we possess the image and characteristics of our creator, and so He calls us His children. But our lack of faith and understanding make us settle for poverty, addiction, immoralities, corruption, and contaminated views of ourselves and all that is around us. This is sad.

We are so beautiful inside, and so powerful, that with our minds and what they can bring to pass, we can create our own environment. It is clear that how we see ourselves is what we are going to replicate. Now can you imagine when we begin to see ourselves as we truly are, so beautiful and unique, and begin to replicate that? Imagine what our neighborhoods and our nations would look like! Imagine what the people who live there could become! And all because of how we perceive ourselves. We make decisions every day and every moment of our lives. When we don't know who we are, we make more bad decisions than right ones. But what I want to make clear is that there is a righteous feeling within us, every time we make a decision to pursue our destiny. It feels right, it feels hopeful, it feels fulfilling. It seems like we are at peace with ourselves. These are the feelings we must take heed of when we feel them.

I must add that I'm not speaking of the emotional feelings that we usually get when we are with a romantic partner. Destiny and a meaning of life is something that's already inside *you*. It cannot be given to you by another. I am talking about the positive emotional urges we feel deep within our bowels the moment we step into something new, whether it be a school course, a seminar, a surrounding you found yourself in, an action you took, a book you read, or even a song you heard. Do not ignore such nudging. Put aside all else, to the best of your ability, and pursue it. Who knows? What you just stepped into could be a gateway to what will unleash the greatness within you.

One cannot ignore the fact that, every time we indulge or participate in something that's not going to get us anywhere, but, rather, will take us a step back from where we should be, we feel disturbed and even filthy. This is a good indication that we are heading down the wrong path and should turn away from it. The reason some people don't, in spite of all the nudges , is because they have participated or acted upon it for so long that their nature has now accepted that what was wrong is now right for them. And this can lead them to a great downfall from destiny.

I have often been in a place that gave me a taste of my destiny, and gone back to my old environment, people, and culture. This usually chokes off every good thing I felt in a seminar or a book I read. This is normal. If you think about it, how can you empty out a huge closet full of old clothes, then replace it with just one suit or pants? The closet would still look empty, wouldn't it? Of course! The answer to this question is really simple: You have to gradually keep adding new clothes as time goes by. As you are able to receive or purchase more clothing, you keep adding to the closet until you fill it up again, but this time with *new clothing*. This same principle applies with us. Even though the old mediocre principles are thrown away, it takes the consistent learning of positive information to fully replace the old with the new. What we must know, and should keep feeding ourselves, are the same things and activities that stimulate and provoke the inner-greatness that lies within every human soul.

There are many occasions in our lives when we just take what we can get or what has been given to us. This world and just about everything that's around us have taught us to settle. We settle in our relationships, at our jobs, at school, in our ministries, with what we buy, and with what we eat. Most of the time we do not settle because we want to but because it's "what we can get." So we settle for it.

The individual who's tasted destiny, though they've accepted what they've been given, will never settle. In any and every given environment, they want the best of everything—from friends to their spouse, their career to just about everything they're involved in. They could be broke and in major debt, or the last person considered in a group—it doesn't matter. Even if they have failed on multiple occasions, they will not be moved to simply settle for what *seems* like "all they could get." A taste of what they might become will have consumed their souls and hearts. They are constantly meditating on it, and they will keep feeding themselves with it. People will mistake them as selfish, consumed with themselves, but the truth is they're not. They are likely to be more compassionate toward others than most. They have simply felt something that could change their lives, the lives of those they love, and the lives of those in their circle of influence, for the better. This is where true discernment can be found, for many will scorn and forsake the individual just because their perception of them is distorted by their own stagnant way of thinking. The moment an individual with destiny in their sights begins to think outside of what those other people cannot comprehend or understand, that individual becomes an outcast, a vagabond, a traitor, and a waste of time. But when a taste of destiny has been conceived, no opinion or man-made perceptions can hinder the one who's pursuing it. You see, the single human being consists of a personally divine calling and a purpose that is distinctly for them.

All they need is within them, so when they are being scorned, humiliated, hated, or rejected, they could not care less about who is with them and who is against them, for opinions and criticisms thrown at them are like balloons thrown at a wall: They just bounce off.

Note: A taste of destiny is like eating your favorite meal with your bare hands. Once you've tasted it, you can't stop licking your fingers until it's done.

At times when we hope, we do so only because of something we've seen: a business, a house, a car. That's all good, but it's not going to sustain you when you're ready to make the jump, at a place of doubt and worry. That sort of hope is easy, but it doesn't sustain you. You have to hope mostly for what you *cannot* see. That's the definition of hope, in a nutshell. It is easy to hope for what we can see. The real nugget is to hope for what we cannot see: a better personality and character, a new life, a good future for your family, your financial freedom, for the lives you haven't touched yet... We should train our minds and hearts to ignore every impulse to settle and to chase after whatever we feel deep within us. Though you appreciate the job, the gifts, the kind gestures, the life of being able to just get by, this doesn't mean you should ignore the feeling of wanting to chase after your destiny.

What one must do in this stage is embrace (and begin to make room in our schedule for) the hope, and feed the seeds that have been planted to awaken their purpose and reveal their destiny. What we feel can either be a blessing to us or a curse. In the society we live in, we have the tendency to tend, care for, and caress the bad feelings. The difference between those of mediocrity and those who are living fulfilled lives is that those who are fulfilled tend, care for, and caress the good feelings within them, and that awakens their greater self.

People who have had a taste of destiny cannot stop daydreaming and thinking about what their lives could be like if they were living with purpose. They daydream in the shower, at work, in the car, at home, on the road, with friends, and in some cases even when they are out on dates. You wonder why most daydreamers don't have long-lasting relationships (chuckle)? If the point of a solid relationship is to lift up the other higher than yourself, and you seem to drift away to the Lalaland of your future, your significant other will likely start to be suspicious of you, and to think that something else is more important to you than they are. Either let them become a part of your dreams, or take on the impossible task of containing yourself while you're with them.

The choice is yours, but you cannot ignore your dreams or put them in a box. Your dreams are sometimes all you have in this dark world. They don't betray you. They are closer to you than any other. They are personally attached to you. They go where you go, they are where you want them to be, they end up where you want them to end up, and they rest where and when you want them to rest. They are our best friends and a great source of strength. Though all men dream, those who dream by night in the dusty recesses of their minds wake in the day to find that the dreams were only vanity. The dreamers of the day are dangerous and unpredictable individuals, for they may act on their dream, with open eyes, to make it "possible" or even their "reality." Our truest life is when we are in dreams wide awake.

Many have negative impressions of dreaming, but you can dream positively. Just be ready to act upon them. Happy is the individual who dream dreams and is ready to pay the price to make them come to pass.

The power of imagination makes us infinite. We must first learn to always tell ourselves what we could be, and then to do whatever we have to to become that person. Go confidently in the direction of your dreams and take no detours. If you're on a detour, get back on track and follow the road set for destiny. Live the life you have always imagined!

As I've mentioned, our truest life really takes place when we are dreaming while awake. So, it's time those dreams wake up, and become a reality. Do not be one of the walking dead, who look alive and yet are not living! Walk toward your dreams with your eyes wide open, and you will see the path that was made for you.

Note: A man with no dreams and aspirations is like a broken-winged bird that can never fly.

Note: A man with dreams is like a baby eagle waiting for its opportunity to soar.

Our daily struggles and challenges have a way of suffocating everything we aspire to be. Sometimes, we just need some time off, with a series of pleasant thoughts that will distract us from our present situations. There are those who will call you insane, but the truth of the matter is that daydreaming, for the individual chasing after their dreams, is completely sane. There is nothing wrong with it. We just live in a world where people have it backward. They consider what's *not* supposed to be normal "normal" and what *is supposed* to be normal "insane." The human mind was built to create and bring to life the secret imaginings that consume our thoughts—imaginings that nobody else knows about until they come to fruition. We must accept the fact that, in this harsh world, sometimes we need to step out of the darkness of our present "reality" and into the sunshine of our dreams. We need to swim in the sea of our beautiful imaginations, and breathe in the peaceful air of a brighter tomorrow.

In a life full of chaos and uncertainty, we occasionally need a healthy dose of daydreaming to remain sane in this dark world. One must come to realize that, over countless generations, daydreams have become totally misunderstood and misinterpreted. We have come to see daydreams as false entities, made up by our own human imaginations. This was never meant to be. Let us agree that it is not the daydreaming that's the problem. It is the character of the individual who is daydreaming that we must take note of, for you can either be carrying the weight of the world on your shoulders or daydreaming about what you will strive for in life. What we must come to accept and see is that the circumstances, situations, afflictions, and difficulties we face every day are actually the false narratives that we humans have embraced throughout time, due to the programming of our mediocre thinking, making our now unhappy and unfulfilled states real in our lives.

We should make the commitment to ourselves that our current situation, circumstances, and difficulties are what's false and only temporary, while our dreams, goals, and aspirations are what's real and what we should work toward, focus on, and eventually bring to pass.

As we dwell in the circle of our dreams, we become drawn to anything or anyone who has walked or is walking in something similar. We will search for books that they wrote or influenced, listen to songs and audiotapes that they made, pick up on their every speech, admire the way they carry themselves, go to their seminars, take their advice, and much more. It is often not that we actually want to be like that actual person, but rather that the lifestyle they live, the message they are bringing, the people they influence, and the character they portray are what motivates and remind us of what we want to be. An individual who's had a taste of what they could become is very alert and sensitive to anything that reminds them of what they could possibly be.

We are not robots, but living beings who are sometimes robbed by our surroundings, which present to us so little to work with. So, in the light of seeing anything that reminds us of our dream, we instantly become drawn to it. When not cautious, this can sometimes make us very vulnerable, and we must be careful that we don't end up in bad situations or with bad people whose purpose of situations have been misconstrued. Just because some things or people remind us of what we could be like, that doesn't mean it's always safe to associate ourselves with such influences. The fact that it reminds us of what our tomorrow could be can be enough.

I've seen people who ended up trapped in bad relationships, bullied and pushed around, degraded, manipulated, used, and discouraged. These things sometimes happen because we focus more on just being around someone than on learning from the experience that brought them through. We also often make the mistake of getting involved with people we admire but forget why we admire them. We fail to check their character before jumping in the pool with them, just because we think we like them. Do you know how many young men and women have being abused and used by celebrities they admired? I'll leave that topic for another time.

We must understand that, at times, even though someone has made it to a point they sought to reach, the principles they applied to their journey weren't based on good morals or integrity but rather on lust, greed, and manipulation. We should always be alert to a person's characteristics, rather than just their fame or fortune. Just because they "made it" doesn't mean they did it with integrity.

One man is not responsible for another man's success, but we look at the examples and experiences of others and then take lessons from their journeys, good or bad, for making our own dreams a reality. For example, there are many examples of those who have died and left a great legacy behind them. When one sees themselves becoming a president, they might look at Abraham Lincoln or Ronald Reagan, or a freedom fighter who acted with integrity and love, like Nelson Mandela. Someone who aspires to become a great intellectual might look to a great counselor, author, or teacher, like the great Dr. Myles Munroe, or great orators like Winston Churchill or Martin Luther King, Jr. Someone wanting to possess great compassion might look to people like Mother Teresa and Mahatma Gandhi. The world is never short of examples, both past and present, from whom we can learn. We just need to find the right ones, observe their life, learn from their experiences, discover their motivations, and apply them to our own lives. Learning from someone who is, or has been, where you want to go can be one of the greatest sources of knowledge and inspiration for achieving goals and bringing dreams to pass.

We've noticed how people adore Hollywood actors and actresses; some have elevated them to a place of royalty, acknowledging and even idolizing them. Even though I'm not really mesmerized by Hollywood, it's hard to ignore the way some people act when they come in contact with their favorite stars. They want a signature, a photograph, their questions answered, and sometimes even a hug. I've seen people collapse when they see their favorite stars. It is remarkable how some people can idolize others so much that they lose track of who they are themselves.

There are multiple issues with idolizing others. As I mentioned earlier, it is good to see someone achieve something and learn from their experiences, but idolizing another person, to me, seems a clear indication that the individual is very much unaware of who they are themselves.

By idolizing someone, we give that person status and power over us, like a god, whether we like to admit it or not. Sometimes it's a matter of low self-esteem, but idolizing someone is putting that person into a position of inflated pride and negative self-worth. In a natural sense, both parties can be destroyed internally, whether they are rich or poor, and not even know it.

Someone who's really tasted their destiny is too focused on what they're going to become to be mesmerized by others. Their hearts are already fully occupied with what they've discovered about themselves, and have no room for anyone else's "glory." Sometimes, people who idolize others are empty and broken in their hearts, and are just looking for a person of status and fame to rub shoulders with, in order to feel some level of importance themselves. This goes beyond Hollywood and right into communities, neighborhoods, friends, and family. People just admire external beauty and appearances. There are those who idolize others just because they love their movies or careers. There are also those who just plainly hate their personal lives, and by idolizing others, they (in some small way) make the lives of the individual they idolize their own.

There are many other reasons why people idolize others, and though it's not always motivated by a negative quality, we must come to the conclusion that it is never good for one human to idolize another. Instead, they should simply take the positive lessons from the experiences of that person's journey and apply it to their own life, in order to get closer to where they want to be.

People who've had a taste of destiny tend to ask many questions of themselves and those around them. The thirst to understand what's bubbling up in them makes them very compulsive. When they cannot get answers, they examine their experiences to see if they can find answers there. They go back to incidents, situations, circumstances, and events from their past to find what they seek. They have the tendency to look deeply into things that occurred. Others could be looking at the same things, but it's impossible to see the answers to life's questions there. One who is searching for answers, however, has eyes that can see through life's worst and bring out the ingredients that are lurking in their experiences and those of other people.

They will search their childhood—every crevice and loophole. They will even go as far as to examine the stages in life where they experienced their greatest extremes. The triumphs and failures and heartbreaks they went through during their school years—experiences that came to prove and prune them—will all be investigated by the urge to discover who they are, unafraid of returning to some of the dark clouds that once shrouded them.

Having defeated some of these past demons, they are eager to know what tools they subconsciously used that helped them. Personal experiences, for these champions (or young eagles, as I call them), are the greatest teachers.

When they have tasted their destiny, no experiences in their present life will go unnoticed or overlooked. They will live a life of awareness, highly observant to all that is occurring in their life. They will have come to understand that their greatest teacher is much closer than they had perceived. Experiences at work, with friends, and family, with the circumstances and situations they bring—every instant of their life's journey—will be absorbed by these young eagles, desperate for answers. They know what to cherish, what to preserve, what to adore, and what they don't want to accept, which they quickly flush down the toilet, lest it contaminate their destiny.

The taste of destiny can do remarkable things for people—emotionally, naturally, and spiritually. Having an idea of what they could become helps them make all-around better decisions in their lives: what books to read, who to listen to, where to seek advice, what to heed and ignore, what company to keep (and what to avoid). In spite of how difficult life can be at times, the individual who's tasted their destiny tends to live their life with appreciation and contentment, especially when things are not going so well. They've grasp the fact that, though their eyes are fixed on the glorious prize at the end, it is the experiences before the end result with the road map leading to it.

People who've tasted destiny are always looking to find someone who can explain what it feels like at the top of the mountain. They can be very nagging, desperate to know every bit of information. They are the ones who can't stop talking about their goals and aspirations at barbecues, dinners, and family get-togethers. If they are quiet, it is because they are listening to what's going on around them, trying to see where everyone is at, or thinking of what their next move is going to be. They are so focused on what the future will look like after they fulfill their dreams that, no matter how bad their current situation is, it doesn't affect them at all. Sometimes, these people can be going through a great deal, carrying a lot of weight in life, and managing a lot of pressure—but from afar, they seem unencumbered. They've seen the beautiful fruits hanging in the garden of their future destiny, and are determined to get there at any cost.

Note: Just as a bulldozer moves every bit of dirt on its path, so is a man that is chasing after his destiny.

The future is bright for the individual who wants to take hold of the opportunities to become all that they can be, with the will to overcome all the challenges of their chosen path. The one who's tasted destiny knows that there is no end in trying, and failure is only an indication of what did not work; they just keep moving. For someone who's tasted destiny, the sunshine always penetrates the vision of their imagination, just as it penetrates a dark living room with open windows. There is no ending for these individuals. The only end is the grave. For even after they make it, the will to always keep moving gets so strong that they use what they've achieved, big or small, expressing great creativity in order to keep building and growing. Their steps and decisions in life are often not understood by family, friends, or co-workers, not because they are arrogant or stubborn, but because they have not beheld the vision of their own dreams; not the way the misunderstood individual has. They've seen it, and now they're going after it. Get out of their way or they will move you!

Note: Destiny will embrace the individual who's living in it, even when they've not touched it.

Note: People who've tasted destiny tend to live in the future of their imagination.

People who've tasted destiny have the tendency to see what they're going to become and so begin to dress like it, walk like it, live like it, talk like it, act like it, eat like it, and often even spend like it. I should elaborate a bit on that last item. Those who've tasted destiny are not spendthrifts, but they like to look good, wear fine clothes, drive a beautiful car, and live professionally. It is not that they are boastful or trying to show off, but the excitement of what they've envisioned is so strong that they want to know what their expected end will feel like.

Of course, it is inevitable that they will learn things along the way about dealing with money—but make no mistake, they will try (to the best of their abilities and with all integrity) to live the life they've envisioned. As a part of their journey, at this stage, they would quickly learn the discipline and maturity needed to manage money. They often love to talk like the person they've seen themselves becoming. They will try to develop that level of speech. They will listen to those they look up to, apply their speech patterns and styles to their own, read books to improve themselves, and go through dictionaries in search of words that could help them become more eloquent. Their training is non-stop.

For some, the closer they get to their goals, the less hungry they become. But not for these people. The closer they get to their destiny, the more persistent they become. They don't mind driving a beautiful car here and there, and eating in fine restaurants if they can afford it in their current state—though that's not what motivates them. It helps them a little mentally and emotionally, reminding them of what their future will be like if they persevere. They might be broke, but believe they have money. They might be in debt, but believe they are going to pay it all back shortly, and in cash. Their circumstances could be very bad, but though they live in them, their state of mind is not there with them. They always feel like they are the ones to make a difference. Every decision they make is influenced by the individual they see themselves becoming. They could be fired at their job, jumping from one location to another, just out of a relationship. They may have been deceived, robbed emotionally or physically, be in debt up the roof, or the everyday target of a nasty boss. They might have kids to take care of, with rent overdue, a shortage of food, and a health problem that seems to affect them time and time again. But despite all these obstacles, these destiny-driven people feel like all is well, because they think, feel, and live the life they see themselves eventually living, even though their current situation is telling them otherwise.

CHAPTER 9
THE RIGHT NORMAL

There are normal things we've come to embrace or accept in our lives. Some are so normal that we don't even notice them: having children, going to school, loving our children, spending time with friends, educating ourselves, finding a good career, taking care of our loved ones, driving a car, going to barbecues, and so on. All of these and many more are just basic normalities of human life.

In this chapter, these are not the normal activities and ways of life I'm going to be discussing. Instead, I'll focus on the negative and positive emotional behaviors, habits, traits, and personalities we've embraced in this culture of ours, things that could either destroy us by keeping us in the shadows of nothingness, or remake us into vessels that can transform our lives and the lives of those around us.

I want to start with the negative aspects of what we've come to know and accept as normal. Many of these things are not really for our benefit, but are just methods and systems we've been brought up with or introduced to. Not many people in our circle would, or could, tell us that these principles are not healthy for us, because everyone has been victimized or is being victimized by them. The signs and proof of some of these negative normalities are all around us, but we do not have the necessary discipline and discernment to see or pick up on them. Only very few grasp it. Sometimes, the voice of these signs can be so loud that everyone in their surroundings hears it. Others who grasp them leave to go and find a better life of their own. Kudos to the ones who choose to remain and make a difference. As for the ones who leave their people, after discovering their new revelation, well, you can't really blame them for wanting to get out. We can only pray that another with much more integrity will discover this truth and make a difference for all.

Now let's break down some of these normalities.

Negative emotional normalities

Emotions are any relatively brief conscious experiences characterized by intense mental activity and a high degree of pleasure or displeasure. In saying this, imagine what type of displeasure we put ourselves through based on negative emotions. There are emotional tendencies that make us feel sad, mad, frustrated, grumpy, critical, or otherwise awful, just to name a few. We are subconsciously blinded to these sorts of tendencies, on a daily basis, only because they've become the norm in our lives. They've ruined relationships, jeopardized careers, destroyed neighborhoods, shut down communities, closed businesses, made wars, inspired murders, caused divorces, and much more. We've seen our parents and others before us working tirelessly, causing depression, broken homes, stress, anger, un-forgiveness, resentment, bitterness, and hate. These emotional reactions cause more damage to the human soul than anyone could imagine.

But because we have seen those around us expressing these emotional reactions, we overlook them and eventually they became the norm to us. It is normal to get a divorce, it is normal to be angry, it is normal to hate, and not to forgive, it is a normal thing to get frustrated. We've created so much mess within us, which was never supposed to be normal, that it is now the norm, to the point where we think something is wrong if these emotions don't occur. *Destruction and misdirection only fall on the human being based on the false ideologies they've accepted to be true.* There is nothing normal about these deficiencies! As we conform to this type of emotional negativity, it spreads like a virus to any and all those around us. We humans have interpreted the usual to be full of turmoil, darkness, difficulties, and shame; sadly, most of us live our lives expecting these things to happen. This ought not to be so!

How about we look into some of these emotional deficiencies that have become the norm to us, and talk about the effects they bring in their wake?

Frustration: This is the feeling of being upset or annoyed, especially because of an inability to change or achieve something. This emotional reaction is a great indication of insecurity, insufficiency, dissatisfaction, or wanting. We always dismiss this as normal. "Oh, he is just frustrated."

By dismissing this as "just" frustration, we fail to look at the cause of the reaction, and overlook the brokenness the individual is undergoing. Frustration can come in different stages, from the basic, temporary state to those states that linger and fester, leading to things like murder or suicide. Every negative emotion I've mentioned, when ignored, gets worse, opening the human heart to receive more of the harm it's causing, often leading to horrendous consequences.

Anger: This is an emotion that tells us when something may be wrong. For example, we may feel angry when something is beyond our control or feels unfair, when we can't reach a goal, or when we are hurt or threatened. We can also be angry when we are under too much stress. The danger in anger is that it can involve a wide range of feelings. It can be invited in with something as simple as the wrong gesture or comment. It cannot be underestimated or taken lightly. Anger can also occur when a person feels their personal boundaries are being (or are going to be) violated. It robs us of the ability to process things and issues properly. It steals our will to judge correctly, and buries the wisdom to make wise choices. Anger puts everything good within us in a choke hold.

This emotional expression of it can be simple or extreme, and I don't need to explain how far that can go. Anger has a way of making us lose control of ourselves and every sense of discipline we've adopted. You can be calm at one point, and in an instant can be the mean green Hulk. We know that we've all expressed some form of anger, whether it be minor or major.

Those who pick up on it early tend to break from its grip before they do any real harm to themselves or those around them. Sadly, we've taken this negative emotion and accepted it in our lives, making it the norm despite where it leads us.

Depression: This is a state of low mood and an aversion to activity, and it can affect a person's thoughts, behavior, feelings, and sense of well-being. People with a depressed mood may be notably sad, anxious, or empty. They may also feel hopeless, helpless, dejected, rejected, or worthless. Depression also produces symptoms of guilt, irritability, or even anger. Depressed people might also feel ashamed and restless. They may lose interest in their family and friends and in activities or programs they once considered pleasurable. They might experience a loss of appetite or begin to overeat. They may suffer problems concentrating, remembering general facts or details, making decisions, difficulties in relationships. Depression can even lead to attempts of suicide, successful or otherwise. We consider depression fairly normal. It often doesn't occur to us to look into its causes before it is too late, and we are at a funeral, sadly wondering what we *should* have done.

Un-forgiveness: Un-forgiveness is a disease that, when not tended to early, will not only contaminate the person but also become a walking virus contaminating everything else around it. Alexander Pope made a statement that I find very fitting: *"To err is human, to forgive is divine."*

This is a truth that still resonates in our hearts today. Forgiving others seems to be one of the hardest things we ever have to do, but forgiveness is not for the individual who has offended us. It is for ourselves. "Forgiveness is a gift we give to ourselves."

It is difficult at times to face the wrongs that have been done to us. Most of us deny, even to ourselves, the severity of our wounds, which makes forgiveness almost impossible. In other cases, we are well aware of the hurts we've experienced, and believe the offender should suffer some consequences for what they've done. If we forgive, it seems we're letting the culprit off too easily, and we don't want to encourage repeated offenses. Also, our ability to trust others is being challenged and possibly destroyed. It is eroded with each hurtful incident. We tend to think it is wise simply to write the person off, or to avoid them as much as possible. In that way, we can protect ourselves from the possibility of further pain.

We may carry the memory of offenses that date all the way back to our childhood years. Your parents may have rejected or abused you. Maybe your mother preferred your sibling over you, because they were more attractive, or perhaps your father tended to hit you first and ask questions later. You might be in a marriage that requires you to forgive your spouse daily, though every feeling of love, intimacy, and warmth has disappeared. Should I mention the injustices we may have felt at the workplace? Passed over for a position just because of our gender, race, or ethnicity?

Un-forgiveness is so normal around us because the life we are in offers us plenty of opportunities to feel unforgiving. What we should realize is that the lack of forgiveness does more harm to us than the offender. When we don't forgive, we grow hardened, mistrustful, and bitter. We want the person who wronged us to suffer. As a Christian, I know that these negative feelings war against the love and compassion that should characterize me, and if allowed to continue, will eventually hinder my spiritual growth and maturity. That is a fact. Un-forgiveness, unlike the other feelings, is very hard to detect because it is secret and internal. It is buried in the deep cemetery of one's heart, and you'll never discover it until you decide to reveal it. That's what makes it hard to help individuals with such an issue. This negative emotional reaction has become such a norm in our lives that, instead of fixing the issue, it feeds it. We share it with others who are like-minded, which adds fuel to the fire.

These negative emotions, and many others I've mentioned, are not to be encouraged, accepted, embraced, or tolerated. They are an abomination to our soul and a cancer to our hearts. Though we know this (most of the time), our human tendency to consider them normal is very high, seeing it all around us. In this broken world with broken people, we need internal healing in order to be free of such strongholds.

As I've mentioned, that we repeatedly tell ourselves these deficiencies are normal is definitely a good indication that our world is broken to the point of self-destruction. They are not normal! We have simply made them so!

Normalities in daily challenges

Let's touch on some other normalities, such as difficult situations, circumstances, incidents, or any of our daily human challenges. We consider it normal to miss our bill payments, because we lack financial freedom, saying to ourselves, "Becoming financially rich is only for a chosen few." We consider it normal to work two jobs all our lives in order to make ends meet. We consider it normal to live in poverty. We consider it normal to be single parents. We consider it normal to struggle day by day. We even consider it normal to live life always just trying to get by, just surviving. I ask myself: when will this all end? These sorts of things continue to happen not because we cannot change them over time but because we have accepted them to be the norm, and that's allowed us to embrace what we weren't supposed to. In life, it is inevitable to go through certain things that will try to keep us unproductive and weary; that is life. That is life. Difficulties will arise only for us to tap into our inner strengths to change them. The discipline and ideology that we must learn to embrace is that we must learn, study, persevere, endure, and overcome in order to get out of the circumstances and situations that have become the norm for the majority of people.

I wish I could change the situations and circumstances that I see some people going through on a daily basis, but I can only do so much. The individuals need to speak to *themselves*. "Enough is enough! I've had it, and now I need a change!" Not much change can be done in the individual's life until they reach this point, no matter how much you try to help. They have to want the change first before anything can be done. Life was never given to us to be miserable, confused, lost, or living in poverty. Sadly, this world has made it to seem so.

Normalities in addictions

Note: The addict will make an excuse for a drug in order to justify themselves, only because they are addicted to it.

Different sorts of addictions can also become normalities. I've seen people high on marijuana, crack cocaine, heroin, meth, ecstasy, and more. One thing that never seems to surprise me is that, whenever one mentions quitting to an addict, they bluntly explain to you why they think the drug they are addicted to is not that bad.

I ask myself, "How can you realize something is bad for you when you're still bound by it?" Only those who are sober can see the effects of the drug on the individual, whether they like to accept it or not. Now, to go back to my point of the normality in it, people who are addicted to a drug generally started off very small. After taking it consistently over a period of time, it becomes the norm for them. Common sense should tell them that what they are doing is harmful for their minds and bodies, but that sense is locked away by the addiction itself, keeping it imprisoned until the human will to get out says, "enough is enough." These people started off having control over the drug; then, as time went on, the drug began to have control over them. This is why we call it "addiction."

Note: Negative habits and addictions only seem right or normal when the culprit has engaged in them to the point of no return.

Another form of addiction I'd like to stress is alcohol. This is one of the most common addictions we know. In my life, I've seen people do some weird and foolish things when drunk. I'll name a few: Walking through red lights, hardly able to stand on their feet while cars are going by, having to slam on their brakes lest they hit the drunkard. Getting into arguments and fights that can result in lifelong injuries or fatalities. Ending up having a one-night stand that leads to an unwanted pregnancy. Going into dangerous, wrong places at the wrong times, risking being abducted, kidnapped, or even raped, because you weren't fully conscious and able to make stern and wise decisions, thus giving a predator the upper hand. I've seen people drinking so much alcohol that they become abusive to their spouses and loved ones. Others have drunk themselves into laziness and unproductivity in their lives, using the addiction as a way to help them avoid the thought of their failures.

Should I mention the sad reality of seeing homeless men who ask for money to buy alcohol, rather than asking me for food or shelter? It is a sad thing that this is the norm for some people. They've come to believe that life cannot get better outside of whatever it is they are addicted to. These should not be considered normal ways of life, only they are for those who've made them so.

The truth is that this world has made drinking and alcoholism a way to temporarily forget everything that is happening in our lives and just having fun for a moment. Sadly, some folks never return from such a trap.

Another addiction I definitely want to touch on is the addiction to sex. This is the addiction most known to man. As we grow into adulthood, it is a normal tendency to desire a romantic partner. Sadly, the process of respect and integrity in the act of sex has been so demoralized in our society that it's been perverted and used to satisfy the lust of an individual rather than to express love, connection, and intimacy between two people, leading them to produce children, and continue on a beautiful legacy with decency and good morals. Our sinful human tendencies have contaminated this divine act between romantic partners, and have now invented such atrocities as adultery, fornication, and all sorts of sexual immorality.

Sex in marriage is a good thing for both partners, but it can also be a curse to those who are addicted to it. It'll cause you to lose respect (for yourself and others), take part in immoral activities, rape, assault, feel jealous, commit pedophilia, and sometimes even murder. Addiction to anything is bad, but addiction to sex can lead one to contaminate themselves to the point of violating the character of their human soul and body. It knows how to bury integrity and dig a cemetery for all that is called humanity.

As a teenager, I myself was involved in relationships with the opposite sex, jumping from one to another, addicted to sex, and responding to just about every urge with the opposite sex. After becoming a Christian, I've learned to respect my body and the body of the opposite sex. I came to the understanding that women are someone else's daughters, and that they, too, can be hurt emotionally and mentally. Realizing this, I've applied good morals and basic biblical principles to my life, which has helped me to be celibate for about thirteen years, since my conversion as a God-fearing Christian, and led me to the writing of this book. I'm not planning (nor am I willing) to give up that level of integrity and way of life until my God provides me with a wife—a woman I can call my own and the mother of my future children. No temptation will change that. We've all made mistakes—this we know—but we ought not to remain in those mistakes. Instead, we should allow those mistakes to make us better, as humans.

Others have made a sexually promiscuous lifestyle out to be the norm because they are addicted to it, or *want* to be addicted to it. It is clear that they simply don't want to give it up. But if I can do it, anybody can do it. It begins with the understanding of what sex really is between two individuals, which in return will lead you to start respecting your body, and waiting to choose the right spouse to share it with. But now, immorality in sex and the addiction to it have become so common that even a good thing like celibacy or "sex after marriage" is considered odd.

I must add that, for generations, Hollywood has played a big role in deceiving us about what intimacy or sex really is, promoting everything from pornography to counterfeit relationships. What a sad state our human race is in.

Normalities in traditions and culture

It is normal for us, as humans, to follow the traditions and cultures in which we were brought up. But it is one thing to follow these and another to do so when those same traditions and cultures are hindering us from ever achieving something that will change our lives for the better. I am of African descent. My parents and those before them were born and raised in the far west of Africa. They later migrated overseas, which led to me been born there. When I was about five years old, my parents took me to their home country of Sierra Leone, where two generations of my father's family were born. We stayed for about five years.

In those five years, I learned that the habits expressed by people overseas were based on the traditions and culture they adopted during their childhoods in Sierra Leone. After the five years, we immigrated to Canada, where I've also come to understand and adapt to the Canadian culture and way of life. Even though I've lived in Canada for over twenty-one years now, I've seen and been introduced to different traditions and culture throughout my life.

We keep traditions to remind us of our heritage, history, reunions with families, and to keep order and respect between siblings, elders, or even nations. But destiny, my friends, has nothing to do with traditions and culture. For destiny is not something we were born or raised into, with respect or adherence, like traditions and culture, but it is, rather, something we were born with, embedded within us in the womb by a divine entity. Traditions and culture, if not observed carefully in any given environment or organization, can easily be a stumbling block in one's pursuit of their destiny.

An individual with maturity and personal discipline knows when to separate traditions and destiny, balancing them both in order to achieve amazing results in their lives. Success can sometimes require us to give up some things we had been brought up to think were right, and then learned were really not. Making that decision, between traditions or destiny, can be a challenge.

Traditions, customs, and culture can be so normal to some individuals that they become the source or the focal point of their decision-making. This can become self-destructive, when an individual has made their traditions and culture masters over them, bringing them to their families, friends, businesses, ministries, and communities, and spreading the virus that buries destiny and embraces the past failures of another. Traditions and culture can be so normal that those who have been victimized by them don't see any other way but that to which they have been introduced and raised to believe.

I'm grateful for Canada, and the environments I've been placed in, challenging me to look past traditions and culture and embrace destiny and purpose. I'm grateful for a country that shows people opportunities and the potential of what they could become. I'm grateful for a country that leaves one with no excuses to fail, having created an environment in which anyone can succeed, if they so choose. This is Canada, and the country I've grown to call my own.

Though my family and I were raised in different traditions and cultures, I've learned to balance the two. My background and the five years I was in Africa showed me the traditions of my African heritage, but the one I've grown into celebrates the traditions and way of life in North America. Though these two totally different continents have both contributed to my growth as a person, I've grown into the North American way of life: confident, bold, tenacious, courageous, determined, and having the will to become something.

Despite experiencing all these traditions and customs in different places at different times, I've learned to separate them from my decisions around my destiny and purpose. Though I do not have much knowledge of what my African heritage is now, I do know that the blessings, education, and experiences (both internal and external) with which my God has provided me in this country called Canada have given me the opportunity to step out of what is considered the ordinary and into the extraordinary. I love expressing some of our African traditions with my many family members, including siblings, cousins, uncles, and aunts, and I delight in being with them. But I know when to differentiate between traditions and my God-given purpose. Different nations all have traditions and cultures to which they are connected to. What we must realize, regardless of race or creed, is the importance of knowing when and how to balance traditions and destiny, for they are two different worlds.

Positive emotional normalities

Just as there are negative emotional normalities, there are also positive emotional normalities. Our surroundings and society have taught us to believe that negative emotional states are the norm, and, frankly, in many cases, they are. But there are other people whose normal is not negative in any way. Whether they are emotional or not, the decisions they make on a daily basis, and just their perception of what life is and what they represent, are very positive and goal-oriented. Though they are the minority, many inventions, motivational books, songs, big businesses, successful organizations, and so on, were founded or brought to life by these types of people. The daily disciplines that they had to undergo and the criticisms they encountered were no different than what we face every time we're about to step out of the box of mediocrity or what seems normal to others.

It will be good to touch on some of the things that awaken these people, what stirred them up, what makes them tick, and what inspires them. We know they've been scorned, humiliated, rejected, despised, forsaken, betrayed, and ridiculed. And yet these men and women say, "No matter what comes my way, and no matter what they throw at me, I'll keep on moving, anyhow!" There have always been people like this, and their positive emotional thinking has led to inventions, creativity, books, songs, businesses, ministries, and so on, some of which are still impacting us to this day in spite of the fact that they passed on long ago. Let's touch on some of the positive emotional normalities that can lead to such productivity.

Joy: This comes from the experiences that are delightful and memorable, when you feel that everything is right, when you feel happy (despite any form of negativity that is going on around you), safe, satisfied, and comfortable. It is a feeling of great contentment and pleasure that lifts up the spirit.

Hope: At certain moments in life, you may experience some problems, difficulties, or challenges, and feeling hope means that you know all those issues are only temporary. It means you feel and believe things will change for the better, and that the future is bright and beautiful.

Cheerfulness: Feeling cheerful means you are in a state of mind that is positive. It means you are optimistic and happy.

Enthusiasm: This is the emotion you'll feel when you are extremely excited about, or very interested in, something.

Pride: When boastful and feeling superior to anyone else, pride is negative and will easily lead one to their demise and downfall. That's not the pride I'm talking about here, as a positive emotion. The pride I'm talking about here is the emotion that comes from feeling the importance of what you are doing, or are a part of, and exalted for the things you achieved or are currently engaged in. The journey of where you started and where you are now successfully and appropriately brings about a level of pride and respect for yourself. When you have achieved something great, which is considered as valuable in social terms, you will be proud of that achievement. Feeling proud has a positive impact on your confidence.

Awe: This is something that happens when you see or experience something truly powerful and great, and when you are completely stunned by all that greatness. For instance, it may come from seeing things like an impressive work of art, a beautiful sunset, some part of nature, an entity that's unlike any other, and even the fruits of your own labor coming to fruition.

Contentment: This is the emotion you'll feel when you're satisfied and happy, when your mind is at ease.

Enjoyment: The pleasure felt experiencing, having, or doing something you like is called enjoyment.

Inspiration: This is a feeling inspired by an uplifting experience that basically takes your breath away, such as watching a sunset that is simply perfect, being the witness to excellence, and more.

Satisfaction: You will usually feel satisfaction after you fulfill a certain desire or need, but you can also feel satisfied when you help someone with something.

Admiration: When you feel positive about people who are skillful, talented, and exceptional, you admire them. It is a positive social emotion, and is not something to ignore.

Surprise: When you do not expect a certain event, which is pleasurable and desirable when it happens, and it does, you'll be pleasantly surprised.

Interest: Every human being has the desire to learn new things and see new places. Humans are always curious and eager to explore. When you feel interested in something—a person, a place, and so on—you instantly become more open to the adventure and the experiences you'll discover and learn about.

Kindness: This often involves affection and warmth. This emotion is about being considerate, generous, and friendly to other people. The world we live in today does not have much of it. Most people think only of themselves and not others. This is a major problem.

Euphoria: This is the emotion you feel when you're deeply overwhelmed with an experience that involves a great joy. For instance, you may be euphoric when you begin to see the signs of your hard work and the success that is coming to you.

Amusement: Life can be full of humor, funny stories, jokes, and playful experiences that will make you laugh very hard. One should take advantage of these moments, and feel completely amused, for you do not know when you're going to have one again.

Serenity: Serenity is similar to joy, and often stems from it. Because you feel that everything is right, that feeling is followed by tranquility and peace of mind. It is being in a state where you feel relaxed, don't have any worries, and are completely calm, just enjoying it.

Gratitude: This is about appreciation for certain things and people in your life, such as good health, great friends and family members, talents you might possess, gifts you have, fortune, fame, and so on. Being thankful for it all.

Confidence: Believing that you can do something, that you can accomplish your goals, or that you will successfully finish a particular task.

Love: This is my favorite and most powerful of all, for if all else fails, love will never fail. Love conquers all. As important and valuable as all the other positive emotions are, love is (without any doubt) the most frequently positive feeling. Moreover, love is an emotion that includes many other emotions and feelings, such as interest, awe, gratitude, joy, and more. It is an extremely strong feeling of affection, and it is the feeling that makes people feel good and happy, and makes life as beautiful as it is. Love keeps families together, tightens relationships, sustains marriages, builds trust, moves compassion, and is the source of worthy leadership. It is in everything. Even in us. We just need to learn to tap into it.

These are the emotional normalities we must embrace and apply to our everyday lives. In every human, no matter where we are in our lives, we can use either all of these positive emotions, or just the one(s) that fits our current situation best, in order for us to get ahead and not be overcome by the darkness that seems to currently overshadow us. Rather than listening or adapting to the negative emotions and ideologies of what we've being taught are OK and normal, we must try to exchange the rotten fruits that negative emotions bring for the succulent fruits borne of positive emotions in order to reap some of those blessings.

It is very difficult for any human to adapt to all these positive emotions at once, making them a constant and normal way of life, but that doesn't mean that we cannot apply most of them. In my case, I always love to use the one my current situation or challenges demand. Whether I've attained it or not means nothing to me; what's important and will be remembered is the positive emotional tool I need to use or apply in order to get me over the hump at that urgent point in my life. When you are consumed with hatred, un-forgiveness, or any other weight that holds you down, counteract it with a positive emotional reaction.

When you feel like giving up, that's the time you need to persevere. When you feel like all is lost, that's the time you need hope. When you feel like you have no more ideas left, that's when you activate your faith. When you feel like all hell is against you, that's when you bring forth the greater within you. When you feel like there are giants in your way, that's when you awaken the sleeping giant within you. When you feel like you are all by yourself, that's when you realize that, even with no physical help, all you need is already with you, in you, and all around you. When you feel worthless, stir up self-worth, knowing that you are unique and special in your own way, and that no one can do *what* you do *like* you do it.

The point off all this is that negative emotions *will* come at all stages of our journey, no matter how hard we try to avoid them. So, let that be our signal to counteract them with a positive emotion, at all costs, lest we fall into the pit that we've subconsciously dug for ourselves. One cannot reach their destiny and fulfill their God-given purpose while carrying around all the negativity they've blindly embraced throughout their lives. There are demands associated with changing the bad circumstances in our lives, and those demands require emotional changes, mental changes, spiritual changes, and sometimes even physical changes.

It will not come easy, for everything that you've been taught, and all the emotional deficiencies that have being embedded in you from your youth that do not fit the script of your purpose in life, will definitely be challenged and overthrown by the necessary demands of your true calling: your destiny. This then makes it very hard to overcome and pass through the fiery path that we all must take in order to see the beautiful result and who we really are. If there is a change that is required in my behavior, attitude, or belief system in order for me to get to the my God-given purpose, I've learned and come to understand that it must be changed, no questions asked. Period!

This is my character. This is my way of thinking. This is my attitude. This is my way of life. This is my destiny.

This is my RIGHT NORMAL!

CHAPTER 10
DISCOVERING IDENTITY

The beauty of identity is like nothing else. The satisfaction of it is like a drink to quench your thirst, or a peaceful walk across the beach. It feels like shade in the blazing sun or a cool breeze on a hot summer day. No matter how we put it, self-discovery, learning who we are and what we are born to be, is the epitome of fulfillment, for it holds all the answers of one's life. When we think of beautiful, we usually think of beautiful families, homes, cars, land, clothes, and so on, but nothing is more beautiful than an individual who's discovered their God-given identity, calling, and purpose in life. We live in a world that's full of people who are searching for their purpose and meaning in life, ending up at the wrong place, or with the wrong people with whom they try to identify themselves.

That is why the world is where it is today. It is violent, and people are misdirected and misguided. In all creation, isn't it strange that it is humans that have the most difficulty discovering who they are? When I open my eyes, I see flocks of birds knowing they belong in the air, lions owning their pride, leopards resting on a tree as a safe haven. How can it be that, of all these creations, and even as the most unique of all, most humans are either living in poverty, in debt, or are even worse off, homeless or drug addicted? Whether these circumstances are self-inflicted or we are forced into them by others, all are the result of (and stem from) a lack of identity. The beauty of identity is the right of all people, and it is the responsibility of each individual to discover theirs.

Note: A man with an identity is a mastermind at making decisions pertaining to who he sees himself becoming.

The beauty of discovering identity cannot be matched. It is not about how much money you have, the resources you possess, or the opportunities with which you might be surrounded, it is about having fulfillment in understanding your being, gifts, characteristics, traits, personalities, and how the world and what you're surrounded by is divinely built for you to exercise your abilities. The world, and the many incomplete purposes within it that are yet to be fulfilled, is the perfect playground for an individual like yourself to exercise your identity or calling in life. It is very rare for the beauty of who you are or your identity to be given or shown to you. It has to be discovered. The beauty of discovering your identity is that it brings about a level of respect for yourself, an appreciation for how you look, how you talk, what you do, what you represent, who you associate yourself with, and the kind of things you are personally passionate about. You are satisfied in life not because of external possessions but because of what you possess within yourself, and the wonders and glorious attributes within you that are priceless. The satisfaction comes from knowing that when they begin to come to fruition, they will bring about a life for you that is like no other.

I would love to reference some of our greatest leaders in order to get my point across. I wonder what George Washington felt when he knew that his gift and abilities would help him lead a nation. I wonder what Thomas Edison felt when he realized he had the potential to be one of the greatest inventors of all time. I wonder what Mother Teresa felt the day she realized that her life's meaning was to value the lives of others more than her own. The leaders of the known free world, both past and present, all came to realize the beauty of their identities, and that a world was made for them to exercise and maximize on what they'd discovered of themselves and felt like they were born to do. *Greatness cannot be achieved outside of what one has discovered of themselves.*

We live in a world that is filled with the ideas, sacrifices, and inventions of people who discovered their purpose and identity in life—people who were able to make the necessary sacrifices in order to richly express what they discovered to the world.

Note: The joy in one's discovery of their God-given identity is the beginning of a life that is going to be lived with meaning.

I see some people try to find joy in materialistic things, like houses or cars, in the friends they keep, the careers they have, etc. But joy is not found in external things; it is internal. It comes from within. If an individual is not at peace within themselves and with who they are as a person, if there is no joy inside them, it is impossible to find it outside of them. But, when one discovers their God-given identity, there is a joy that cannot be quenched. You become very happy in life. The circumstances you face on a daily basis don't move you, people don't change you, opinions don't hinder you, criticisms don't affect you, and nothing frustrates you to the point of anger or hatred. More than that, you do not stress over life's challenges or misfortunes. Joy within oneself is a wall of protection against anything that comes into one's circle. This is the main benefit of discovering one's identity.

I knew a homeless man once who thought there was nothing left in the world for him. After more than ten years of being homeless, he began to attend programs in the shelter where he would go for food and clothing, about getting more out of life. He loved those seminars. Time after time he would attend them, and eventually preferring them to rushing out to find food. I guess he realized something within him that was much hungrier than the natural part of him. Though he did not notice it immediately, the man subconsciously began to change. His state of mind began changing, and as it did, his appearance and attitude toward life did, too. One thing led to another, and he soon found himself in school studying engineering. He got more scholarships than the schools could afford to give him, and he finished the top of his classes both in college and university. The homeless man, and those who walked past him every day and gave him change, never knew that he was gifted in math and engineering. Then later, he was employed by a major engineering company. Now he is finally settled and secure.

I asked this formerly homeless man how he did it, and he said, "It was not the realization of my knowing I was brilliant in math, it was not the scholarships. Heck, it wasn't even the career I found. It was the joy I found within myself in those seminars at the homeless shelter that helped me to realize that there is something special within me, and because I found that joy within myself, it helped me to be open to stretching myself, and finding my identity." This homeless man found his life because of the overwhelming joy of what he discovered within himself, and the identity he learned to embrace.

I knew a single mother with two children who had to work two jobs in order for her and her children to get by. Two failed relationships and making the wrong decisions at the wrong times led her to the predicament she was in, with two children to care for. She had a gift, though, to motivate and uplift others. She also had a gift of making other women's hair look good. She did it naturally and found joy in it. On her one day off from both her jobs, she would have friends over, and her joy was in motivating them and doing their hair. One of her young children gave her an idea to open a salon at her small apartment, where she could motivate people and do their hair at the same time.

She took heed of this advice, which came from someone who was not even old enough to understand anything about business. Women began to show up often to get their hair done. Some loved speaking to her and getting their hair done at the same time, and others just loved to be around her. Soon after, she had to leave one job, and not long after, the other job, as well, in order to meet the demands of her growing client base. She quickly began training and paying others to do what she did in order to keep up with the number of clients showing up on a daily basis. Her business eventually grew so much that she had to rent a place, and now it's one of the most successful salons in a growing community. I spoke to this woman about her success, and very simply, she said, "My

young boy right through my teenage years, I searched for some
belonging. Trying to find some form of identity, I would hang out
e wrong crowd—thugs and gangs, leading me to have problems
e law because of acting as they did, talking like they did, dressing
y did. It felt like I had found something—an identity and a family
call my own—just by associating with people who looked and
ke me. I learned that the more dangerous and fearless you are in
ets, the more respect you get. Living in a very bad neighborhood
help my situation. It took a lot for me to be able to understand the
nal and mental captivity I was in.

asn't until I became a Christian and a man of faith, genuinely
y good Christian and biblical principles, that my state of mind
y of thinking became totally transformed for the better. Though
ocess of adjustment was long and arduous, I became a whole new
Changing my mindset was one season, and then there was another
and many other seasons after that, one of which was dealing with
who didn't commit crimes, but instead looked for followers, and
who hadn't discovered their identity yet to bring them into *their*
identity in order to affirm their *own* personal man-made status
dership over a particular group of people or congregation. Many
the trap of following these sorts of so-called leaders, and remain
nderneath their psychological control for many years. There was a
my life when I had to break from this form of leadership, because
ons, dreams, and revelations I had received about who I am and
am called to become didn't align with the principles and way of
g that these leaders were trying to implement in my life. I had to
ng, both mentally and emotionally, in order for me to break from
m of mind control.

nging how we dress, how we talk, and how we walk, whether we
ng or it is who we really are, is no comparison to the change in
nds, for that is where the true change begins. When the mind is
d, everything else will follow, whether internally or externally. My
s given me an understanding of what I am, what God has called

joy is who I am, and what I always loved to do k
doors that I never thought possible. Now my c
paid for and their lives are going to have a much
I had." Joy within oneself can lead to the disco
vice versa. It can lead to a life of freedom and in
to remember, though, is that it's all happening v
hundreds of thousands of stories very similar t
If it can happen for them, it can definitely happ
who you are in a world of misdirected and misgu
joy of discovering your identity is so rich that i
that is going wrong in their life and find those li
right, allowing them to be the blessing in their li
rejoice, even when your circumstances are telling

I've made many bad decisions along in my
dealing with the consequences of some of them.
siblings and I knew that we had a loving father, o
was distant. He was not around to speak to us,
and give us answers, protect us, direct and gui
of a father up close, mentor us, watch us, guide
and high school, or anything else. It was just nev
children of my father (of whom I am one) grev
after another, one home after another. Our lives
hoped that we would receive the love from our
father would leave us with) that our father would
of the time, we didn't. It wasn't in them. They w
father was around, but when he left, it was a total
prospered from the money our father would se
and leave us only just enough to survive. It is har
identity when their moving every year from one k
with different individuals, personalities, disciplin
enthood. Psychologically, this makes children gr
and emotionally dysfunctional, not to mention
everyone. My siblings can speak for themselves. /

I was a
type of
with th
with th
like the
I could
talked
the str
did no
emotic

It v
living
and wa
that pr
person
season
leader:
people
form c
and le
fall int
stuck u
point i
the vis
what
thinki
be strc
that fo

Ch:
are ac
our m
chang
past h

me for, and though the purpose he gave me has cost me friends, family members, jobs, and even ministries, I am truly grateful. Discovering who you are and what you are destined to be can usually lead you away from what you thought was good for you but truly was not. I've been in ministries that I had to leave because the methods, systems, and protocols that were instituted and forced upon the people (myself included) were suffocating my purpose and keeping me unproductive and unfruitful, so I found myself remaining stagnant, and no different than the leaders I was following at that particular season of my life. I was able to break free of the emotional hurts I had accumulated as a child, moving from one place to another, growing up without both my parents, living as an outcast and a thug in my early and late teens, trying to discover who I was and what I was born to do in my adult years.

I came to a conclusion on the day of my breakthrough, when I discovered my identity and the God who gave it to me. I found myself, and my past experiences, all made sense. In discovering my identity, I was able to take all the experiences, trials, and challenges I'd faced throughout my life and use them to my advantage, in order to get on the other side. In my identity, I discovered that no one is the master of my fate but me and the God who is responsible for me. As such, no opinions or criticisms move me or hinder me. In my identity, I've now learned to understand that bad circumstances don't arise to break me but rather to *make* me. In my identity, I've discovered that everything I need, in order to be the best I can be, is already within me, In my identity. I've learned that I need not try to fit in anywhere, or try to meet another individual's approval or expectations of what I can or cannot do. In my identity, I've learned to choose my own environment and the types of people I should associate with, whether they appear to be good or not. In my identity, I've learned to not accept, receive, or embrace any perception of me that is not aligned with what my God had shown me of myself. In my identity, I've learned that I don't need anyone to assure me of who I am.

I know who I am. I'm a child of destiny and purpose, and have overcome many challenges that were supposed to destroy me—physically, mentally, emotionally, and spiritually. But I'm still here and alive for a reason. I know who I am, my friends. I'm a young man destined for greatness. The question is, do you know who you are?

It is easy to make the right decisions when you know who you are. You can choose the right spouse, the right career, the right associations in your life, and what to support and what not to. You can choose when to be patient and when to get up and start moving again. You can choose the direction you want to take in life, and the thoughts you want to conceive and the ones you want to throw out. You can choose to overcome the most challenging situations that arise along your path.

The key, my friends, is knowing your identity, for by knowing who you are, your identity or the reason for your existence, all the life decisions you make will be aligned with the beautiful revelation of what you have come to know of yourself. This is the God-given identity, friends! And it is beneficial for all mankind to come to this discovery.

By discovering our identity, the path ahead of us is made clear and the one behind us, that's full of questions, is answered. Let me explain:

Note: Visions and dreams will come, but the man who knows his identity has the upper hand in making them a reality.

By saying that your path in life is made clear, I don't mean that everything will be gravy, calm and steady, full of laughter and comfort. If everything were that simple, then how would we be able to distinguish between the champions and those living in the curse of mediocrity? Challenges will come, afflictions will arise, circumstances will be difficult, and hindrances will stick their big heads out. But the individual who knows their God-given identity knows what has come up against them at any given moment. Their positive state of mind will not allow anything or anyone to break them, or what they've seen themselves becoming. While others look at afflictions as torment, those who know their identity see it as pruning. When others say the journey is too long, those of identity see it as a preparation stage. When others feel pity for themselves in their bad circumstances, those of identity see an opportunity to discover things about themselves they were never aware of. And when others are blinded on a daily basis, just going through life as everyone else does, those of identity are alert, focused, and awake to everything that's around them, in order to find something or recognize an opportunity that they can use to get out of the norm.

Most times, the challenges and difficulties we face on a daily basis have hidden gems that we, in our human nature, fail to pick up on. We are so sensitive about our own comfort that when anything that threatens it, we lose it, and focus on trying to get it back quickly, rather than observing the difficult situation and becoming the masters of it. We tend to respond emotionally and have a breakdown, bringing about fear, stress, and depression. Isn't it strange, sometimes, how we humans can consider what is bad good, and what is good bad? Though difficult circumstances seem like they are there to break you, and often will (according to the ideology of the individual), the individual who is purpose-driven and knows their identity has a way of turning turmoil into triumph. Their vision of what they see themselves becoming, and the end result of their precious life, is so evident to them that they see the secret gems in every situation they face. Similar to scientists, they've envisioned themselves as projects, and the experiences they face every day as experiments to test them, in order to exercise and bring out their fullest potential.

So, they don't see their future the same way as those of mediocrity. Those who know their identity perceive that they are already successful. Failure is not in their lexicon, and there is no intention of stopping. They just keep on going till they're in a place where their dreams become a reality. Their path is made clear, because they have the advantage of knowing the direction to take and the challenges that will come with it. As such, they embrace those challenges—not because all is sweet and dandy, but because they can see what is waiting for them on the other side of that rough and rugged mountain.

You can give an individual who has discovered their identity anything, but if it doesn't align with who they are, even if you assume it's a good thing, they will reject it. Not that they are trying to be mean or rude, they just won't take any chances on things that might hinder them, keep them stagnant, or even distract them. The truth is, when we are on a path toward greatness, there are always things we receive from people that are more distractions than anything else. For example, long ago, I knew two parents and their young son, who was brilliant in school, did well, and got straight As. He was a focused and well-mannered child. The parents were so proud of him that they began to get him all kinds of toys and video games. As time went by, the boy began to spend more time playing with his gadgets than studying and focusing on his schoolwork and the things that were making him better. Not long after that, his grades begin to drop drastically.

The video games he had been playing at home—mainly war and fighting games—had turned him into a menace at school. The boy that had been positively influential turned into a distraction for other kids. At first, the parents didn't know what to do or what had happened, but they later realized that the very things they had offered him as gifts, to show him their love and appreciation, were what had destroyed their child's excellent performance and jeopardized his ability to achieve great things in the future.

What am I trying to illustrate with this story is that sometimes what is good is not really good, and we live in a world that is full of many so-called "good things." An individual who has discovered their God-given identity has the wisdom to distinguish what's good (beneficial) or best for them and what is not. Their IQ and knowledge of where they are in life are very strong, and because they are cautious of every decision they make and what they accept, they minimize their mistakes. The world would be in a much better state if we had more people who had discovered their God-given identity.

After we've discovered our identity and the potential that is embedded within it, and began to reap the rewards of our expected end, it's normal to receive criticism, jealousy, hatred, scorn, rejection, etc. So expect it. When you have reached your goals, overcoming the odds and being and becoming the best you, people will start to cling to you, and many for the wrong reasons. Luckily, by this time, if you maintain the discipline you attained through your trials, these people are no longer a danger to you. But there are those who will hang around you because of who you were, and who you are becoming is so attractive that it is contagious. When you speak, they will take heed. Even if you're making jokes that are not funny, it will be very funny to those who are attracted to you and your achievements. They love the way you dress and how you walk, and the things you're fond of. They hate what you hate and love what you love.

Most importantly, they will try to follow your footsteps, at every step of the way. When people who were never goal-oriented begin to hang out with you, they will begin to adopt your personality and the traits that developed throughout your journey. They will take on your success-driven personality, and your will to be all you can be will start to attach to them. Just as negativity can be contagious, so can positivity be. This is where communities can change, where addicts can start to want to be free, personalities can change, mindsets can be transformed, and characteristics can evolve from impossible to possible.

It is hard for some people to envision the possibility of achieving great things, but as they behold the success of one they knew, someone who went from being at the bottom and worked their way to the top, they, too, will be begging to see those possibilities for themselves, embracing the chances of a better future. They will not adopt everything at once, but their strong will, now embraced, will keep them going long enough for their minds to change, and start to become successful. Whether people are going to hate you or love you, your success will be attractive to their natural eyes, even to those people who wonder why you aren't them. It should have been them and not you. You don't deserve it. They will assume they have endured more than you have, so they should be blessed and not you. Then there are those who will say, "I want to be like that." They will want to know every step you took, every challenge you faced, every choice you made, and every obstacle you overcame. They will want to speak to you at every opportunity. They will admire you and want to be just like you. Being around you will motivate them to want to achieve something, as well.

Whatever the case may be, positive or negative, people will be attracted to your success; you just need to be alert and discerning at all times, aware of the motives of the people who are drawn to you.

Note: The contagious spirit of one living in purpose carries enough weight to change bad habits, communities, and nations.

There are also those who will be attracted to what you've become but will not want to do the same things you've done. They will be satisfied with just being around you, for in it they will find satisfaction. The feeling of being with someone with some level of importance makes others feel a level of self-worth. To a certain extent, there is nothing wrong with that, but, sadly, because their motive is based on their emotional satisfaction, their anchor will not be able to hold on for too long. Soon, they will slide off and fall back into the same circumstances they were always in, *because success is not based on feeding of the energy of another to get ahead, but rather by being motivated by it in order to feed the energy within you.*

It is inevitable that at the peak of your success in anything, you'll attract different kinds of people. Some will come to harm you, others to steal from, manipulate and deceive you. Some come just to rub shoulders with you to reassure themselves of their own importance, and others to learn from you. Be alert! Don't be mesmerized by the attention, love, or anything else that people bring, for some will be using it just to get into your circle so they can see you fall, or discover a weakness in you that they can work with. Remember your past afflictions, challenges, and obstacles, and the difficulties you've overcome in order to get to where you are. These are your greatest friends and your best tools, because they will always be with you. Do not be distracted by fame, money, or status of any kind. Always remember that they did not get you there. Though it is OK to enjoy what you've achieved with friends, family, or people overall, never let your guard down at any moment, for the carrier of your downfall will try to enter through any loophole they can manage to squeeze into.

On another note, doors of all kinds will be open to you—doors you never thought possible. All of a sudden, it is yours for the taken. The opportunities will seem endless and the road of a prosperous future will shine before you always. Everything you touch will be blessed; your actions and efforts will not be wasted. Some of those who never wanted to partner with you or did not see the value in doing so, will suddenly want you to join them on business deals and opportunities that brings about growth of any sort. This is where you'll shine in all that you do, from the wisdom you've attained through experiences and the success-driven abilities that are already embedded within you. This is the point one reaches at which they become the change that people need, and the influence that communities and nations deserve. All these positive fruits of labor begin with the understanding one gains after "discovering their God-given identity."

CHAPTER 11
THE CHAMPION WITHIN

Note: The acts that one expresses on a daily basis are no more than what they've already conceived within themselves.

Within every human lies our true nature, characteristics, and personalities. Some we were born with and others we develop through our experiences or the influences of a particular surrounding of a place or a people. Some have within them darkness that is too hard to even comprehend; others are full of hate and discord, and wherever they go it seems that conflicts and divisions follow. There are also others who are so full of self-pity that they end up either in poverty and other sorts of misfortunes. There are those who are so full of greed that they put everyone else second or last, prone to scorn, and push everyone else aside in order for them to get ahead. Some are so consumed with the desire and will to have power over people, or even nations, that they would do just about anything to attain it and hold on tight. These and many more are only a few expressions of that which is conceived from within an individual.

The human nature is really very simple to understand. You become what you've conceived. If you've conceived failure, then you'll fail at all you do. If you've conceived righteousness, then your actions will pertain to that. If you've conceived hate, then your actions will be based on hatred. And if you've conceived adultery, anger, malice, confusion, discord, or any other negative aspect, then all (or at least most) of the actions you take will relate to those aspects, all conceived within you. The problem is not really that these internal attributes are bad for the individuals themselves; the main problem is that people who embrace them tend to justify their actions, having come to accept and think that this is who they are, when in truth, it is not.

There are other people, though, who are full of attributes that affect their life and their surroundings positively. They have a go-getter mentality, do not settle for less, make positive things happen even in negative surroundings, never stop moving, are always active, do not accept failure (and neither are they moved by it), and keep on going till they get it right according to the visions and plans they've set for themselves.

There is so much positivity within them that it is contagious. At times, it will look like they are smart and full of strengths, but the truth is that they never stopped trying to learn and improve themselves so they could reach their goals, whatever they may be. They are special, not because they are better than everyone else but because they value and see themselves as much more than what was revealed to others on the surface. This group of people are called "champions," and within them lie productive and amazing attributes that are always pushing them, and telling them that there is more to their life than what people see.

I've seen non-champions get stuck in unproductive and bad environments or situations only because they chose to remain there. But champions are natural-born overcomers. Their intent is to be successful at all costs. When others look at an unsuccessful project as a dead end, they have already seen the project finished before they even start it, which makes it impossible for them to think that it is the end of the road. Unlike most, within champions lie attributes that don't mind the process but are willing to go through it, anticipating their expected results.

When just about everyone else is throwing in the towel, they are just getting ready for a fight, and that's the mentality with which they enter the ring of life, at every round—even the last one—with the same motivation and will to win as they had in the first round. They persevere, especially when things are really bad. They are never intimidated by people, status, positions, or environments. They are masters of their own situations, their own relationships, their own minds, their own emotions, and their own weaknesses. Self-control and discipline are their forte. Responsibility and concern are simply the way to do things. It is their motto. For them, overcoming obstacles in their way has become an instinctive response rather than something they are *trying* to do. The will and drive to step over their obstacles is just as strong as the obstacle they face. This means that, whatever comes their way, they are prepared for it, and will match their present or future difficulties with the energy required to overcome all their obstacles.

They are the ones you want to put in charge of a company, even though they are most likely busy planning to build their own. Still, they are the ones you want to lead a group of people, a community, a ministry, or any form of organization. They are the ones who are running toward the fire while everyone else is running away from it. Since there are different forms of obstacles that are going to hinder us every step of the way, it is only fair to say that we need people who are immune to failure, and masters at overcoming any challenge. These, my friends, are champions!

Victory for many people is something unheard of. For others it is scorned and pushed aside. There are those who just try to get by with whatever life throws at them, and they don't care about victories or triumph in the different avenues of their lives. Many fall into the deception of thinking, *"What is there to be victorious over in life? Things are just as normal as they present themselves to be."* Sadly, many have fallen so far into the well of nothingness that they cannot see any victories in life. They can't even visualize what it means or feels like to be victorious over something, because they've been in mediocrity for so long.

Now champions, like most people know, want victory in everything in their lives. Some of them demand it. This is not a case in which they wake up saying, "Today I want victories in my life." As good as that sounds, champions are victorious simply because it is their nature to be so. Let me explain. Winning is not something they search for, for throughout their lives they've been fighting, pushing, and doing whatever it takes to be the best they can be, even in the smallest of things. As they grow older, they subconsciously develop a winning or victorious state of mind, to the point at which victory has blended in with their characteristics and personality. This is what makes them dangerous and very unpredictable! What people do not realize is that, when we're born, though we're born with gifts, personalities, and more, we are also full of space in order to receive more learning and education about this world, in order to be more effective in it.

Sadly, because of the influence of negative societies, neighborhoods, friends, and families, we end up filling ourselves with what is destructive to us and to the calling of our lives and meaning of our existence. Now can you imagine falling into the right circle or environment, one that will deposit positive seeds within you, which will grow and complement the gifts that are already within you?

Note: A victorious mentality combined with gifts and talents is like a blazing wildfire that cannot be put out.

It is very rare that you see an individual who has been around the right surroundings right from childhood. In this negative world, we usually don't have the option of that kind of luxury. So, then come experiences and difficult times—challenges that an individual encounters that carry what it truly takes to awaken their sleeping giants. Sadly, many become worse after the fact, for many reasons. Kudos to the individual who overcomes, for they will reap the fruits of all that they've gone through. And in the process, they will develop a victorious mentality that will embed very deep within them. They will be victorious in their marriages, families, work, education, and emotions. And with their characteristics, gifts, and talents. They will be successful in everything they touch, despite the obstacles that come their way. Into everything that they are doing or going to do, they carry a victorious mindset. For these types of people, failure is not an option. They are going to win. These are champions!

There was a great group of guys at a place I worked. Most of the employees there were doing something productive outside of their work, whether for their retirement or just as an addition to their everyday lives, creating assets for themselves and their loved ones. These men and women were very positive and goal-oriented. They were not perfect. Like everyone else, they had weaknesses, flaws, and shortcomings—but make no mistake, they possessed a strong work ethic and the will to get things done and get them done right. I would like to use one of these unique employees as an example in this chapter, of what it means to be a champion. His name was Jorg, and he was an operator at this company. His position was not the highest in the plant, but he was my superior. We took orders from him, and he told us what our next moves would be. If he made a mistake, we all made a mistake. He constantly had to be on top of things, and his IQ had to be very sharp. As an operator, like the other great guys with him in that position, it was on him to ensure that everything worked smoothly. It was his responsibility to see any flaw or danger with the machines and their controls in one department of this huge chemical plant—*before they became a problem*. As such, he had to be alert at all times or be responsible for any disaster that happened to the facility or its faculty. For some people, this is a very difficult job to keep up with, but not for those already programmed to get things done and succeed at everything they do in their life outside of work.

Jorg was in his late forties, a German-Canadian who had lived in Canada for a very long time and made the most of it. He is still doing so. Though he didn't know it, I gave him the nickname "the blazing German Canuck." As a German-Canadian, most of the nickname is self-explanatory, but it was the fact that he was a trailblazer—one who never stops moving and is always looking for the next opportunity that will catapult him to his fullest potential—that accounts for the additional adjective. Jorg was constantly active, constantly in action, and constantly productive—at work and even more so outside of work. While he was in Germany, Jorg's education only went as far as grade nine. That didn't stop him though. He went on to become a chef for three years, after receiving his chef training.

But people like Jorg are quick to jump on the next big thing or challenge in their lives. He went on to join the military. He traveled a lot, taking part in foreign missions wherever he was required. He learned discipline, responsibility, courage and bravery, and applied them wherever they were required. Most importantly, he learned teamwork and the importance of everyone doing their part. He spent four productive years in the military, and learned much. Both the principles and self-discipline he acquired in that environment would later play a major positive role in every avenue of his life.

While in the military, Jorg traveled to Canada on a humanitarian mission. He fell in love with the country, and being the ambitious person he is, he saw the opportunities Canada could provide for him, if he pursued them. Without any delay, he began to work on his immigration papers, going through the legal process to enter Canada and take advantage of its opportunities. With hard work, he knew he was going to succeed. Failure was never an option with Jorg. He said to himself that he was going to Canada and going to make sure he got a job that could pay him twelve dollars an hour. In those days, twelve dollars an hour was equivalent to about thirty dollars an hour today. After patiently getting his Canadian papers, he was eventually eligible to enter Canada and start his new journey. He wasted no time, and immediately went to work.

Though he did not get the immediate results he had hoped for, he had a goal, and he was willing to start at the bottom and work his way up, which is the way of champions. They do whatever it takes, even if that means going into the gutters and getting messy, all the while keeping their hidden agendas very close to their hearts, allowing them to come forth every time they start to forget why they do what they do, limiting the risk of becoming distracted or taking a small detour from what they had originally planned. They are masters at staying focused.

Jorg took on small jobs, working in hotels and restaurants, and he could have stopped there, but he is a champion. His mind was not stagnant. Just about everything he looked at he saw as something from which he could learn, grow, and benefit. So with the experience he gained doing those small jobs, the blazing German Canuck went on to open his own restaurant. He took all the skills he acquired and made them work on his behalf to get to a higher level. And he did not stop there! As his achievements and growth kept adding up, he looked into building more assets in his life, and creating more opportunities for himself and those in his circle. Champions are always looking for the next best thing, and they have the instinct for positioning themselves in the right place at the right time, in order to reap the benefits of whatever is available. He lived in Edmonton, Alberta—"the oil province." At that time, oil and engineering were going to be the next big thing. Our champion quickly picked up on that and was determined to position himself to take advantage of it.

Despite all his past successes, he did not hesitate to keep creating assets for himself. The man, who only had a grade-nine education, decided to go back to school, training and positioning himself for the booming oil business. He continued upgrading his education by entering into "Wardin Well Services." As opportunities kept brewing, our blazing German Canuck kept matching obstacles or hindrances with either a higher level of education or workforce experience, not to mention his work ethic and self-discipline. It was a no-brainer. He went on to enter Nait, a college in Edmonton, when he was well into his adulthood. He took "pre-engineering" and, after graduating from that, "petroleum engineering," at which he was also a success. Not long after, the ambitious, blazing German Canuck went on to add a "power engineering" course to his resume and skillset, and of course, he conquered that, too. By doing so, he had positioned himself mentally and intellectually to take advantage of a situation that was booming at that time.

Then he took on a job at BiWay, and then upgraded himself, becoming a sheet-metal worker. He busied himself even more by taking on jobs at Dan's Foods, Canadian Tire, and MTE Logistics. His personal developments and professional qualities eventually opened doors for him with great companies, like the one at which I eventually met him, where he worked for over thirteen years before I arrived. He did his job very well, and still does, and his contribution is a great addition to the company and his co-workers.

He also owns his own snow-removal and landscaping business, outside of work, called "Bobcat Jorg." This has also been very successful, and he never allowed his responsibilities there to interfere with his responsibilities at work or vice versa. He takes them both on, as well as all his other daily tasks, with discipline and accuracy, getting the right results—doing them all simultaneously and with the perfectionist attributes of a champion.

I am sure that there have been many times in the blazing German Canuck's life when he probably wanted to just throw in the towel, but he has always persevered; it is not in him to quit. He is programmed to observe the environment that he is in, and position himself there for success and a promising future. He is programmed with the mind of a champion. Champions are always looking ahead and always active. They are very proficient at picking up on change, whether with the economy or their own environment.

Like ants, when champions have enough, they store the excess for future needs. Like lions, they hunt and protect their circle, in order to preserve themselves and their loved ones. Like sheep, they are humble enough to learn from those who have made it. Like giraffes, they possess the ability to reach the best of the fruits and leaves at the top of the trees, where no other animals can reach. Like elephants, they know where to dig for water when there is a drought. Like wolves in a pack, they associate themselves with those of like-minds, to stand a better chance of survival. And like squirrels, they are constantly moving and active, doing all they can and working as hard as possible so that, when the winter of life comes, they will survive on the rewards of their labor. Champions don't think twice about their future. They know it's going to come anyhow, and so they prepare for it. So when most people are running around, going crazy and losing their minds because of the changes of life and the difficulties that come with the unknown, champions are calm and stable, not only because they know the difficult times are just a means to improving their God-given abilities but also because they are consistent in their will, asserting and stabilizing themselves before anything happens.

Jorg and people like him are the masters of their own fates. They could care less what people's opinions of them are. They see something, they take control, they execute, and they stop at nothing until they reach their desired goals. Being a champion doesn't mean you have to be a billionaire, a millionaire, or even rich at all. It isn't about money. It is about having the spirit to keep getting back up and fighting, no matter how many times you got knocked down. This is what brings great results. No matter how you want to express that spirit, or what results you are interested in, you will achieve them with the heart and mind of a champion. The blazing German Canuck, my friend Jorg, is a great example of a champion, and there are many others like him. Sadly, not enough.

People always have the wrong perception of what a champion is. Sometimes it's only because they are envied, but mostly it's because the one who is doing the envying is threatened by the champion's work ethic, and human will, and that they can get things done that they feel that they cannot do. So, they scorn the champion, justifying themselves and their own weaknesses in order to hide, making the champion out to be a bad person. But the truth is they are afraid, because the presence of a champion reveals their shortcomings and weaknesses.

Rather than learning from the champion, their pride brings about rebellion, hate, and disregard for the champion. Another reason why people always have to say negative things about champions or people who are purpose-driven is that mediocre people have a way of making champions seem abusive. Let me explain. Champions are always on the go, always active, always thinking, always searching for the next big thing, and always productive. They possess amazing characteristics and emotional disciplines while witnessing all the amazing results come to fruition in their lives. When mediocre individuals, who do not know or want to apply that level of commitment, are around people like that, they can easily make the champion look abusive when they are working on a project or in an environment together, when in truth it's just that they are not as aspired or goal-oriented as is the champion-spirited individual.

If the champion is in a leadership role, and giving orders to someone who's satisfied with mediocrity, the champion will have demands around what needs to get done that the one with a mediocre mindset will not be able to deliver. The champion might need an individual who is willing to do work overtime when required, and can be on standby at all times (whether at home or at work). They might need someone around them to pick up on things they have missed. They might need an individual who is always reliable, and just as committed to the project as they are. They might need all these and much more.

Sadly, when mediocrity is working with a champion-spirited person, they are unable to match the champion's requirements, and so tend to slow down, complain, and not give their all. Worse, it will seem to others around them that the champion is being too hard on them. In truth, no one is being hard on anybody. They are both just being who they are, personality-wise, and no one is changing for the other. You see it everywhere. There is always that champion who likes to get things done and be something in life, to make a difference for themselves and others. And then there is that mediocre person who says things like "Oh, we are OK with where we're at. You are just too much. You are just too ambitious." Mediocre people have a way of making something look bad only because it reveals their stagnant state of un-productivity. I know many champions who are reading this book, and no matter where you are, you have dealt with people of this sort in different places and organizations, and have heard them make such statements. Then again, if you've been living in some level of mediocrity but are reading this book because you want to learn some tools to bring out the best in you, then, my friend, you are ready to go to the next level of productivity in your life. Good on you!

Though Jorg is much older than I am, even old enough to be my father, I can say that I'm truly proud of him and the life he has lived and is living. He owns a few houses, has bought land and other assets, including his own businesses. He is also going to expand his horizons with his next big project. So, I know the best is yet to come for Jorg, the blazing German Canuck, because he possesses the spirit of a champion that pushes him to keep winning at everything he does, even when difficult situations tell him he can't.

Note: The definition of a champion is not based on the achievements of an individual. These are simply the fruits with which champions are rewarded after they get knocked down so many times and just keep getting back up and fighting.

Champions define their own situations, and if they are in one that does not represent how they see themselves, it is only a matter of time before they create an opportunity or get into a situation that best reflects the gem of uniqueness within them. When all others say they have no opportunities or success, champions say, "I'll create my own opportunities, and I'll create my own success."

Note: Champions have the tendency to pick up crayons and color their future with the most amazing colors from their own imaginations.

This, my dear friends, is an attribute that is very rare, and yet it sits right there with the best of all human abilities if we can learn to tap into it.

Champions are like the nutrients of the soil, the life of the party, and the engine that makes the car move. They are the strength that lifts the weight, the source of light in the darkness, and the hope when all seems lost. They will persevere and break through walls if they must. Champions only see failure and dead ends as challenges in order to stir up their creative genius and break through it, creating opportunities when it looks like there are none,

That, my friends, is what makes champions special. And you, reading this book, are one!

CHAPTER 12
EXPERIENCE IS TEACHER

There are many ways of learning or educating oneself to grow profession-ally, intellectually, and as a person. The normal way is, of course, going to school, from kindergarten all the way through to college or university. We also learn things from those who surround us, like our parents, family members, or friends. It is evident that the communities and neighbor-hoods in which we grow up also play a major part in educating us. The human mind, from birth, has to grow into wisdom; though we have powerful minds, with gifts and talents, if we are never put in a situation or given the opportunity to discover and exercise them, creatively and intellectually, we will never be able to be all that we can be.

All these different forms of education are normal, and in most cases, good. It leaves me now to say that, of them, the most important is our own personal experiences. The challenges we face, the afflictions we endure, the difficulties or stumbling blocks that seem to always be in our way, the pain or misery that seem to be the norm in our lives, the emotional education we learn from relationships, whether good or bad—all these are personal experiences that, if observed carefully and handled correctly, can be the greatest teachers in our lives. The worst thing that can happen is to go through life's trenches and not learn any-thing from them. Going through the fire is hard enough, but if you've come out of it with burns, bruises, and scars, at least *take something from it* to better yourself and those who might be going through similar fires. Experiences, though not living beings, are just as alive as the individual going through them. They are what bring out the best, and in some cases the worst, in us.

Note: The character of an individual is best revealed when they are going through the darkest moments of their lives.

These experiences can speak as loudly as one is willing to hear them. They warn us of distractions, they remind us of past failures before they can be repeated, they nudge us before we get into relationships that resemble failed ones, they align us with our path, they give us wisdom, they help us grow and build us in places no psychiatrist or doctor can reach. Experiences are the source and true origin of our greatest achievements. In any given environment, project, or goal, we achieve only because we made enough mistakes to learn what doesn't work and kept looking for ways that might work. If you are one who doesn't make mistakes, I guess this doesn't apply to you. If you're like me, and have made mistakes, you need to learn from them in order to grow. Sadly, many do not.

Note: Experiences, both good and bad, when not fulfilling their agenda to educate, have a way of repeating themselves; hence, taking the individual on a merry go round of similar experiences until they finally get it.

Life is a journey and experience is a teacher. It is not prejudiced to race, creed, or background. It is going to come whether we like it or not. Though experience can be very positive in the world that we live in, it has been a curse for most. Externally, I've seen people living on the streets, in poverty, needy, involved in more than one failed relationships (even marriages), and much more. The external evidence of experience is not learned. It is just the visual results of what happens when we dismiss our experiences, and don't take them seriously. The most dangerous and disturbing of all is what the curse of experiences not learned does to us on the inside. It brings about bitterness, anger, hate, un-forgiveness, rebellion, stubbornness, low self-esteem, insecurity, pride, and more. These negative developments at times go further, and bring about addictions to drugs, alcohol, and lust, not to mention extremes like murder or suicide. People are the most influential in themselves, and if that self-motivated spirit is taken away from them, they fall into an endless pit of shame and regret.

Note: Failure in life is no more than mistakes and bad decisions repeated over time to the point of no return.

This world is really good at letting us know about the challenges we face, the negativity that's out there, and the turmoil that's all around us. But we fail to teach others the benefit of learning from all of their experiences and of breaking the cycle of the repeated generational curses that have infested the human race. We have seen the curse of adultery infesting families for generations, and the habit of men beating their wives passed down through family lines. How about hate, or generations of grandfathers, sons, grandsons, and great grandsons all getting involved in drugs, prison, or womanizing? I need not mention the cycle of unwanted pregnancies through generations of women. How about businesses shutting down, homes being foreclosed? The truth is that life is full of these incidents, and others like them. But however much we talk about these incidents, we fail to learn from the secret "nuggets" of wisdom that are hidden in them, and so repeat them. As such, rather than their being a positive force in our lives, they are a curse.

When our experience causes us to focus on the good ole days rather than the now, they can also be a curse. When you *were* making money and were successful, things just seemed to always go right. You didn't need to put in too much effort in to see results, and everything seemed to just fall into your arms. When tough times came along, as they always do, these people complained about the way things were going and began to long for the good old days' return. They spent more time remembering and dreaming about past successes and didn't focus on present issues. They thought about what could have been, instead of meditating on the creativity needed to overcome present challenges. This form of reminiscence includes all of what life throws at us, even relationships. People caught in this cycle tend to blame everything but themselves, and so their experiences become like a curse. Instead of looking at their situation as a means to give birth to whatever creative ideas might lurk within them, they live in the "now" of how things were.

We've all heard the term "blessings in disguise." As a matter fact, we've heard it so much that we do not think about the term the way it is intended. When we see these disguised blessings, in even some of the most horrendous situations in our lives, we tend to not only make the right decisions at that moment but to find the needed creativity or wisdom to get out of it. And when we do get out, we become a lot stronger than when we went in. Some of these hidden blessings can be difficult to pick up on while all the chaos is going on. The truth is, they are "blessings in disguise" because although they occur in some of the worst situations in our lives—and they tend to bring out the greatness in us. The individual who has the courage to see opportunities in the midst of their misfortunes has the upper hand when it comes to awakening the giant within them.

There are many examples of blessings in disguise, and I'm going to take some time to elaborate on a few. Some of these hidden gems can occur in the midst of, or after, a bad relationship, within families, business, ministries, and more. Our world has a very interesting way of working. We sometimes notice that, while we didn't get what we wanted or expected, we did get what we needed—although sometimes only barely. But that is very hard to see while in the heat of the moment. It's not the end of the world that you didn't get that dream job you applied for. Go-getters always see failure as an opportunity that was missed only because there is a better one waiting around the corner, assuming they can persevere. These people have a way of reaping glorious results in the end, for when one door closes on them, another really does open.

Some people get released from a job, for any number of reasons, and they lose their minds, which is the wrong reaction. What you as an individual must focus on is what opportunity will be available to you next.

What about when a relationship ends? It is never comforting when someone you lived with and shared your deepest secrets with leaves you. You discover that the one you thought you were going to spend the rest of your life with doesn't feel the same way as you do. This can be emotionally devastating. It is very difficult for some folks, even the most positive ones, to see anything good in this. But it *is* better to find this out now, before you've had children or have put so much more into the relationship. Alternatively, there are people out there who have put everything they have into terrible relationships. I am here to let you know that, if you're conscious of what's going on, then you are still strong enough to do what is best for you, and sometimes even what is best for the other person. The truth is that there is someone better waiting out there, who will appreciate you as an individual, or maybe opportunities in your life that will allow you to be more effective as a single person, committed to yourself and your future rather than to an individual who doesn't see your value or understand your self-worth.

In some situations, it is good not to always get what we want, for it brings about humility and eliminates negative pride. If we do make it and become successful, with that sort of pride still lurking within us, the fall will be much greater and harder than having never been in the place of making it at all. After everyone acknowledges you as the prize for every company, the genius in every situation, and the answer to all problems, it is very easy to develop a level of pride. So when you finally come face to face with a situation in which you feel vulnerable, to the point where even your best efforts and wisdom are not good enough, that's when humility begins to form, eventually bringing about good fruits of your labor, and, most importantly, good fruits within you.

It is important to realize that you are only human, and like everyone else, you have shortcomings and weaknesses. Sometimes, the more we focus on how special and unique we are, the less desire we have for our goals and projects. Your personal gifts, talents, and individual uniqueness will get you far, but there comes a point in one's life when you need a lot more than just that. It is in those moments that commitment, a strong work ethic, and your human will can get you over the hump. It's sort of like déjà vu, this self-discovery—seeing something now in reality that you already knew you possessed.

How about the time when all was going well and all of a sudden you got knocked down to your knees? You lost everything you'd worked so hard for, and it seems like all is lost. These are moments in which champions are separated from the rest. It is a very normal thing in this present day to see people fall into a deep pit in their lives. The problem is not that you fall into it, as that happens to most of us at one time or another. The problem is getting back out of there and fighting through. Whether this fall was caused by your own mistakes or the mistakes of others, you must look at it as a means of evaluating everything that has gone wrong, and why it did. This calls on your mental discipline and emotional strengths, as you try to remain calm and access patience. In situations like this, you stand a better chance of recovering when you maintain focus and do not lose your mind.

There are a few more scenarios I'd like to touch on. In life, there will come a time when our emotions, our heart, our own self-confidence, and even our personal knowledge of what we are capable of will be challenged, by being shattered. This is often why some folks have a mental breakdown. Moments like these reveal things about life that others don't see. Sadly, most remain stuck in it. But the brave few who will find a way out of it tend to leave with much more. These individuals are shown what it feels like to be empty, or between a rock and a hard place, and by understanding what it feels like to be at the bottom, they are able to stay focused and disciplined in all that they do, never wanting to go back to the place of nothingness.

I always say that age is not the definition of maturity, but of having gone through difficult times and tough experiences. This has a way of turning "boys into men" and "girls into women." I described some of the changes that occur with the individual in such metamorphoses in a previous chapter: "The Transition."

There are days in your life when you wanted to just give up every-thing and throw in the towel, and yet you held on. You held on, and said to yourself, "I'll make it despite how I feel, and even if I die, I'd rather die trying than remain in a life of mediocrity or keep living a life of just getting by with no purpose." This is the moment of recognition, when you break every obstacle, both naturally and spiritually. Success in any area of life is for everyone, but the reason why there are only a few who make it is *that* moment, when they must decide whether to keep moving forward or just throw in the towel. Striving toward your goals and dreams when all the odds are against you is not an option; it's a must! You are determined to become successful at all costs, even when everything and everyone around you is telling you it's not possible.

It means to press on when it feels like there is nothing else to press on for, because, my friends, there certainly is. You've just reached a point where it's so dark that all you've envisioned becoming seems a little dim, when in truth it's much closer now than it was when you started. In times like these, one must press harder than they ever did before.

These are only a few blessings that can come out of difficult experi-ences in a world that's so vast, and full of pain, misery, and misfortunes. The human race still exists, not because of our past failures and shortcom-ings, but because even though we've being knocked down and buffeted throughout the ages by wars, poverty, bad ruler-ship, and more, we refuse to give up. Our experiences have made us rather than destroyed us. What makes us unique is our ability to learn positive things from seemingly inevitable destruction.

Turbulent times have ways of bringing about some of our greatest vic-tories, creating great leaders, and teaching us personal development. Some of the best teachers and greatest of influencers, both past and present, have undergone some very difficult moments in their lives in order to effectively make a difference or help someone else overcome their dif-ficult moments. Some folks do not realize that *the harder the terrain, the greater the reward.* To help someone look at their difficult situation in a much more positive way is to know that the more difficult their situation is, the greater the reward will be after they overcome it. This system has been in place since the beginning of our human existence.

Note: The more weight you can handle, the more will be offered to you; the level of discipline you can maintain determines how much you can manage.

These disciplines and moments of personal growth can only be revealed when one is in a difficult circumstance. How one handles the pressure in the turbulent times of their lives will determine whether they are ready to go on to the next phase of their lives. It is no different than trying to fight a bear when you can't even handle a mouse. The turbulent times in our lives reveal to the master how much of the sleeping giant within us has actually awakened; then the master will set us in a place where our current capabilities can best be effective, so as to help us (temporarily) so that we might eventually reach a place at which our true potential is revealed and can be exercised.

Most people get it twisted between having to be educated by a normal school environment and having to be educated by experiences. What you learn at school, though it adds to your intellect, will never compare to the lessons you learn through life's experiences. Intellectual learning can be important for your career, profession, and efforts to keep up-to-date with new technology. But it is what you've learned in your life experiences that will help you maintain that position. Though your intellect stimulates your mind, it is life's experiences that show where and when to apply that wisdom. Though intellect can open up doors for you, it is life's experiences that can show you which door to take. Though intellect gives you confidence from knowing your stuff, it is life's experiences that gives you the strength to persevere when things go wrong. People have made it without the intellectual education, but how many times have you seen an individual become successful when they haven't learned from their life's experiences? Education, as I've mentioned, is no more than just an add-on. If one has it, it will build a better you. But the greater teacher is the challenges and experiences one encounters as they go through life's journey.

There are too many of us who are afraid of difficult experiences (rightfully so), but we must come to a point where we learn to perceive experiences as teaching opportunities rather than "just more misery." When we do that, our perception of the most difficult moments of our life will drastically change, and we will reap the rewards of this new level of maturity. It is very important to obtain this state of mind in difficult times, for it is what's going to help the individual think their way out of the mess they are currently in. Some people choke and drown in the midst of their worries, bringing about stress, depression, and confusion. This can sadly lead to drug addiction, a life of immorality, suicide, and much more. Bad experiences, when not perceived properly, have a way of bringing out the worst in an individual. An individual and their experiences remind me of a man and his wife, or vice versa. If you perceive that your spouse is going to be miserable, suffer bad luck or pain, then you'll always be looking for it. It's like you're trying desperately to find in the individual what your negative perception is of them. Having created that expectation and perception of your partner in your mind, you miss out on their gems and positive qualities. Alternatively, if you are constantly seeing the positive aspects of the individual in any given situation, even when their weaknesses and flaws are revealed, you will not be moved by them, because your positive perception will trump how they seem in their current state.

As one allows their experiences to be a blessing to them, they give themselves the opportunity for them to be a benefit to them in their future. We can maintain what we can contain, and we can only contain what we've being proven to know how to handle. Experiences can do that. Our future endeavors and who we are to become are dependent on what we've learned as we go through our life's experiences.

Note: For the stronghold of your present or future successes are very much reliant on the weight of your past experiences.

Past experiences are full of memories of lessons that can sustain us for a long time to come. We learn something new every day. As our imaginations, visions, and dreams get bigger, our challenges become tougher. There are times when some situations might catch us by surprise, confronting us for the first time and forcing us to search within for the creativity needed to get over or through it. There are situations we undergo in life when all we have to do is look to our past and find the memories of past lessons to help us through. One might say, "Well why not just settle for where you might have no more challenges, being satisfied with where you are?" This selfish way of thinking is one of the reasons the world is in the state it's in. People who are capable of much more are settling for less, either because of the fear of the unknown or the pressure or challenges they are refusing to take on. There are many people at the bottom of the mountain not because of lack of opportunities or creativity, but because it is their choice. *Purpose rarely calls us in the time of our own choosing, but rather has a way of calling us at a time when we would rather be a part of something that requires much less effort and only a little sacrifice.*

We see the mountain and its rough places and choose to remain where it's comfortable at the bottom. We bury the giant within and choose to live with the sloth. In most of these cases, sometimes at the bottom of the mountain, storms would be raging in an individual's life not to destroy them but to wake them up, so that they can keep moving and do something of value in their lives.

CHAPTER 13
COLLIDING WITH PURPOSE

It is clear in the heart of man that there is always much more to life than where one currently is. Many times what we go through in life doesn't necessary explain itself to us. We have questions that most times are not answered, memories of the past that keep coming back to us that we want to forget, hopes that we thought were lost, dreams that seem to be shattered, experiences that seem like they were for nothing, long nights that seem like they will never end, staring at the ceiling, wondering what our lives are really for or what our next move should be, and even how long this situation will last before a breakthrough. Time is the greatest revealer of all truth, and there comes a time in an individual's life, after they've persevered, after the turmoil and difficulties, and after the preparation stages, in which they come face to face with who they are and what they are destined to become. They confront their purpose, who they truly are within, and what they were born to be. This is where man meets destiny, perseverance meets results, hope meets assurance, captivity meets freedom, poverty meets riches, confusion meets understanding, questions meet answers, incompletion meets perfection, lack meets abundance, fear meets courage, discomfort meets comfort, emptiness meets fulfillment, insufficiency meets sufficiency, the unknown meets revelation, weaknesses meets strength, and hostility meets peace.

Finally coming face to face with who you are is one of the best things any human could ever experience. You are not intimidated by your past, present, or future. You now know everything about yourself and to accept the fact that they've happened and you're now moving out from that place; despite what anyone says, you've learned to appreciate who you are. Nothing is hidden from you, and you're not intending to hide anything, only what seems appropriate for you to do so. Experiences have made every crease and pore of who you are evident to you, both internally and externally. Though it takes a while to get used to, the realization of oneself cannot be compared to anything else. You are unique and special all by yourself, and that is definitely something that no one would mind getting used to. You're in environments where your gifts are highlighted, your talents are put to work, and your personal abilities are exercised.

You're not ashamed of how you look or how you perceive yourself. You now realize that you are made in the image of God and His likeness, consumed by His characteristics and traits, fully equipped and capable of becoming anything you are pressed in your heart to be. You are a human that consists of a spirit, soul, and body, bound for purpose and bound to now make a change in any environment in which you're placed. You have now learned to come to terms with yourself, seeing yourself as you really are, accepting yourself and the weaknesses visible to you. You are no longer focusing on other people's weaknesses to feel better about your own. In discovering purpose, you've now come to terms with yourself, knowing that though we are all created by some of the same experiences, what differentiates us is that, through it all, our experiences and life itself have done a good job in sharpening us in a way that fits exactly with who and what we are destined to become.

Now, as you go out into the field of destiny with other champions, you are loaded with your own identity, the attributes required and confidence of knowing you belong there, and there is no doubt that you're going to thrive. Coming face to face with oneself at a place of purpose reveals your true self-worth. Your value is very difficult to notice in a place of mediocrity and nothingness. So as the challenges and experiences came, and as you countered them with everything you could, exercising whatever gifts, creativity, and strength you had left in you to keep on moving, you ultimately understood that your unnoticed value and self-worth had always been there, as it was their unseen presence that never allowed you to settle.

As you indulge in the union between yourself and purpose, you begin to understand more about it. The deeper you get into your purpose, the more you begin to understand the journey itself. By looking back over your life, you begin to anticipate what is in front of you. Now you realize your purpose is not just a means of self-discovery or understanding, but also the pursuit of a journey that has been divinely set for you.

Justifying ourselves and making excuses for not following our path or pursuing our destiny does more harm to us than those the fulfilled purpose would influence. The union between the human and their life's purpose is destined to happen when one decides to take on the journey, by staying on the path despite life's storms, by learning from our experiences, and acquiring a greater understanding of life and how to perceive it, as we develop in wisdom and knowledge.

As I've mentioned before, you've been born to this world containing gifts and things of great value so that the world may be blessed by you, and your purpose is embodied in this project. Because of your spirit, which lives within your body, you automatically have something great to offer the world, and not the other way around. So stop waiting for the world to offer you something. Everything that you are and the divine gifts you possess are hidden deep within you, but they cannot evolve if you as an individual do not advance. Anyone that is full of ego, pride, arrogance, and impatience cannot walk this path, for this journey (when continued) has a way of draining us of all our existing deficiencies. Your purpose in life is very detailed. It's going to involve being around specific groups of people, and specific surroundings or circumstances at particular seasons and different junctions of your life. It is in these periods when our innate purpose tends to reveal itself and allow the individual to discover what they have to give to the world they were born into.

The spirit of the human came from the master and Lord of all. It is eternal and, though the body dies, the spirit never does. It leaves and goes back to its rightful place of rest when its time on this Earth is over. With that being said, your spirit, while on this Earth and in your human body, contains knowledge from its ancient home to bring to this world. When one understands this, nothing can deceive you—not false teachers, not religious organizations, not corrupt governments, and not cultures or traditions. As we allow the purpose of our lives to take course, we begin to discover things about ourselves and this world that not even the greatest minds could reveal.

Your experiences in life have now allowed you to develop a greater understanding of the world and its destiny. Within this context, you will gain an awesome perspective of what your role is in this world and your purpose for being born into it.

Your life was designed to be fulfilled, but the sad and difficult part of it is that this world is a difficult place in which to see it come to fruition. It is certainly not a getaway spot. Neither is it a place where you are sent to be tortured, nor a place you are sent for pleasure. It is a place that needs your gift from the ancient home of the spirit that lives within you. It is for this reason you were born into this world: not to become it, but to save it. Some gifts or purpose-filled lives are not always out there for all to see. More often than not, they are hidden. After expressing or fulfilling them, you will not receive honor or glory for them. This is OK, because you were not given these gifts to be recognized but to make a change. Our world is in great turmoil, and your gifts and purpose are there to make a great difference. Our creator is always at work everywhere and in every dimension, maintaining the world with His limitless knowledge.

God's work occurs behind the scenes. Though we are too ignorant to accept it, it is very active and quite evident all around us if we can perceive it. It doesn't make a show of itself, and so is receiving very minimal resistance and contamination from the world and the cultures it serves. Wisdom and knowledge in the discovery of purpose are similar to that. They work behind the scenes, not looking for any form of recognition, gratification, or glory. What they need is a willing heart and an open mind through it all, in order to reunite with your greater self, which connects you to all life. Purpose is like a good leader who calls on his lost student who has wandered off back into the class of his destiny-bound children.

Too many folks focus too much on creating a fine definition of themselves, when in truth all one needs to really concentrate on is the purpose of their existence, which they must discover. To help with this issue, our experiences and the preparation stages of our lives have a way of helping us to realize this purpose. Many try to make their own way for many different reasons, and in doing so, end up taking detours. Eventually, one too many detours will make you not only lose your path but also forget where it was located and how to get back on it, concealed from life and cut off from the greater purpose of it, which in truth you were born to participate in. Our purpose is not to retreat back to our creator in defeat. It is not to escape the world or justify ourselves for wanting to leave it. Our purpose is to give what we came here to give, and, even more importantly, to bring heaven down to earth.

Note: greater awareness of one's purpose can bring about a greater ability to impact a nation.

Our world is a hungry and very lonely place. It is full of pain and misery, fantasy and false imaginations. Its sufferings seem endless. Its violence is horrendous, and yet its possibilities are great, and whoever is able to see all these things, and realize that they have come beyond this Earth to give something to it, bring about a glorious union between a human and their God-given purpose. Purpose will allow you to realize that you are not here for just any personal reason; you are here to participate in, and contribute to, a greater order of reality that exists in the world, beyond it, and beyond every natural thing we can see with our bare eyes. As you are one with your purpose, you now realize that this calling is not for you alone but also for the sphere of influence you'll be introduced to and the world you're in. As you complete your service to this world, you'll definitely be proud on your deathbed, when it is your time for your spirit to return to its divine home, as it separates itself from the body in which it has dwelt.

You'll return knowing that your gifts were given to the world, and you contributed everything given to you. As the great Dr. Myles Munroe always said, *"You must die empty,"* knowing that you've offered all that was within you. This is the definition of real accomplishment and a life that was purposely lived. To really reap the full benefits of what your purpose truly is, you must understand who God is, what the world is, what life force truly is, what knowledge is, and the experiences that will or have occurred in your life to take you there. When you do encounter this purpose, do not tamper with it. Do not picture it based on your perception and understanding of it, do not editorialize it, and do not pick and choose what to like and what not to like about it. If you do this, you will not be able to move from where you are. It takes a whole lot more than your own human understanding to help you see beyond what your natural eyes can see, and purpose can lead you to that level of understanding.

Life has already become your teacher, as you've learned to discern, communicate, develop wisdom, etc. Experiences will come automatically to play a major role in your life as you maintain a life lived with purpose. From the first step you took in your toddler stages to the years of your prime, you've learned things that have and will contribute to your life of purpose. *"Life has become a great laboratory for the master to bring about one of His most precious experiments: you."*

In the beginning and journey of your life, you had to undergo a season or seasons of undoing. Everything that you believe in, what you admire, what you tolerate, and what you don't, so much that you love things that had nothing to do with your purpose, all of these had to be done away with in dark times, as you entered into a new opportunity consisting of a new mindset and a new way of perceiving life.

The best knowledge that one should come to embrace as they enter into a life of purpose is the desire to be educated and to stop thinking they know it all. Education itself is designed for you to enter new and unknown territories in order to develop and improve for the next challenge ahead of you. It has a way of taking you from the former and into the future, exposing you to new ideas and experiences. This is why education, whether in school or even through experiences, is vital in forming you in preparation of what you are destined to become. Without the education you've received in your experiences, or what I call the preparation stages of your life, it is very rare for to achieve anything. As we know, many people will say that they seek greater wisdom, knowledge, and understanding, but only a very small few will embrace the preparation that comes with it.

There is always something within you that will motivate you to move past your feelings, anxieties, personal agendas, doubts, and fears. Learn to trust these nudges of strength and wait for the giant within you to discover the means to overcome the obstacles. Some of our own personal dreams, goals, aspirations, and fantasies can only get in the way of our living a purpose-filled life, for though they can be good, you don't want to focus on them too much, lest you be drowned by the rewards rather than reap the fruits of the experience.

When you reach a point in life at which you come face to face with your purpose, it is wise to realize that your God-given purpose is not for you alone. As such, do not allow yourself to become self-confident and self-possessed. Your experiences will likely have done a good job of liberating you from the "me, myself, and I" way of thinking, which is good, for true purpose has never been solely about freeing yourself from the trenches of darkness that others of this world have come to accept. It is also about helping others to be free, and, more importantly, helping them to discover their God-given purpose. This is key!

People who have a "me, myself, and I" frame of mind can't really see pass their own greed, fortune, fame, feelings, ideas, emotions, changing behaviors, personal convictions, etc. People like that cannot bring anything to the world but their own confusion and broken ideologies. One of the first freedoms you'll ever encounter is the freedom of your mind, washing away all your old ways of thinking. Your personal mind and its perceptions are totally different than what the mindset of purpose is. This personal-belief mindset is what the world had programmed in people, and when it collides with our purpose, it contaminates it. So, before that occurs, we must help people eliminate that old mindset and adopt a new way of thinking. Purpose is going to free you from the prison of your own ideologies and negative habits, and from the influence of your emotions and personal beliefs. Accepting your purpose will do this in a very peaceful way.

Without a shadow of a doubt, you are going to feel like you were born for this change. It will begin to create new experiences for you, now and in the future, without any associations with past mistakes. This is the time when, as an individual, you must be willing to leave behind all the conclusions about yourself, about who and what you were, and what the facts really are. Most people will choke and feel a level of vulnerability when they begin to experience this change. Others feel insecure and defensive when they enter a place where their control of who they are and what they think they know are challenged and put away.

In truth, this must happen in order for one to move forward. At this point, it is wise for one not to be sensitive to their emotions or ignorant to truth, and to put aside their false perceptions and ideologies of life itself. They need to be attentive, with all focus and humility, and always ready to take action.

Understanding and coming to the realization of your purpose is one and the same with the journey that it took for you to get there. The difference is that, early in the process that leads to knowing your purpose, your state of mind was not at the right place to pick it up or sense it. But purpose has been there all along, leading you, by shaping and directing you through your life's experiences in order for you to reach and understand them fully. It is not some distant goal that one has to reach; it is there with you even now. It is normal, when people think that they are going to become this person or that person, when in truth, you are that person already; you just need to persevere long enough for you to reach the place where it will surface externally, and allow all to see the fruits of what was already in you.

People who succeed in reaching their ultimate self are those who don't just focus on what they are going to become, but embrace the preparation that leads to that place. Your purpose throughout your journey has helped you develop the faith and will to press on, especially when all seems lost. There are unseen entities who guide and direct you, along with the power of knowledge that lurks within the human spirit, though most do not know this (it is true whether they want to accept it or not). Without this knowledge, it is hard enough just to begin, let alone persevere when things begin to go wrong. This is faith at its best: knowing you have help, even when you cannot see it.

Purpose is something that awaits you. It is something that's always there with you in the trenches of life, pushing you, giving you hope, telling you that you can do it, and letting you know that your past is not who you truly are, and that there is more in you than words can utter. Your purpose was designed for you and you alone. It is there throughout the journey that will lead to your discovery of it, in order for you to make a change in your life, and the lives of your family, your community, and even your nation. Your purpose will allow you to give what you are supposed to give, and in this, your life will be fulfilled, because you will be living a life of purpose. As you enter the doorway of your purpose, you begin a greater journey in life, and remain on it in times of happiness and even in times of weakness.

> Do not indulge yourself in the fantasy of trying to be there or making images of what it feels like to be there. Do not remain below in the valley, looking at the top of the mountain and saying, "I wish I could go up there." You have things in you that will carry you there, if you persevere. So instead of just dreaming about it, make that dream a reality. Enter into it. Enter into purpose and live a life that's full of value and meaning, which is your birthright.

CHAPTER 14
AMBITION SUMMARIZED

At last, here we are, at the last chapter of what I hope will be a powerful and life-changing book. It is with great pleasure that I end this final chapter using the same word with which I started: ambition. I have elaborated a great deal on this subject, striving to challenge readers' minds and open their eyes, and I sincerely hope I have done enough to help catapult others into lives lived with purpose, and encourage them to step into their true destinies. I pray that you, the reader, have read this book with the right mindset, characteristics, attitude, and the human will to be all that you can be. And that you now understand a good portion about where you are, where you should be, and what steps you need to take to get you to your expected end, where you can live a more productive and fruitful life, the likes of which you've never seen or experienced before.

One might ask, "What does ambition have to do with some of the previous chapters?" To answer this question, one must define the term "ambition" itself. As it was at the beginning of this book, it is also appropriate for me to define it here.

Ambition is a strong desire to do or to achieve something, typically requiring determination, hard work, and a relentless effort from the individual so that they may reach their expected end. With this definition, my friends, we can wipe out every other negative perception and horrendous description that a world full of mediocrity embraces. For ambition, as some of us know, is not the problem. Whether a particular manifestation of ambition is good or evil is solely based upon the character of the one manifesting it.

As I've mentioned many times, some folks will scorn ambition in general, or the individual expressing it, only because it reminds them of their shortcomings and stagnant state. Because they feel as if they cannot do anything for themselves, they criticize the individual who can, for another person's drive for success only reminds them of their failures.

The preceding chapters have examined everything from the "silent giant" to "the right normal," and you may still be wondering what all of these issues have to do with ambition, although I hope that is not the case. I say this to you, my friends: Ambition is very closely connected to every one of these categories, and very effective at every stage you reach in your life. It is loud, and it is not hard to pick up on. Here is how:

The silent giant

The silent giant is the "greater you" that's lurking within you. When a situation or circumstances in our lives threatens us, our loved ones, or something we believe in or are passionate about, it awakens a powerful force within us, forcing it to stand up, conquer, and keep on moving. It is ambition and the will to persevere that awaken such a giant. It is your ambition that brings you to a place of victory, searches within yourself for internal answers when you can't find external ones, and puts you in a place in life where, when all else is lost, you have no choice but to look within. My dear friends, ambition is the force that provokes the silent giant within you to awaken, as it keeps putting you in predicaments that demand all of you and nothing less.

Hidden potential

There is much to mention in life about one's hidden potential, and I elaborated on the "spirit" that is one of the most important factors hidden deep within man, containing all the gems and amazing treasures of our gifts, talents, and much more. This is our hidden potential, and it can elevate us immeasurably. If the spirit is in one who is devoted to their future, full of righteousness and the will to be all they can be, with all integrity, they have the potential to reach great heights. Now, as we know, the human consists of three entities: spirit, soul, and body. Our bodies are the weakest of the three as they mostly respond to all that the world and the cares of life throw at them. The spirit needs the body to move, and sends direction, guidance, and a map of where it wants to go via the soul, which acts as mediator and interpreter between the spirit and the body. It is the spirit that pushes, encourages, and empowers the human to keep on moving. If ambition is the strong desire to do or achieve something through determination and hard work, then it is only right to conclude that one's ambitious drive comes from their spirit, where hidden potential resides.

Curse of mediocrity

Mediocrity is a place where most people don't want to be. What separates mediocre people from the ones who make it, is that they made the choice not to do anything about their situation, preferring to remain in it instead. Ambition is all over this chapter, for it is the secret force that never allows one to settle for less when they know they can become more, regardless of the internal and external challenges and influences that try to stop you. In fact, ambition is the driving force that opens your eyes to the "curse of mediocrity" and its negative consequences, in order for you to break out of it and do something better with your life.

The transition

One of the most uncomfortable processes the human mind inevitably encounters, in all aspects of our lives, is change. When things change, a transition occurs between what one believed and knew to be true in the past and the discovery of a new truth. It is essential that within this time of transition, one maintain a calm and flexible state of mind in order to adjust to their new or developing circumstances, survive the storms, and adopt new ways of doing things.

The ambitious drive to become better and not be left behind in the darkness of nothingness, with a broken heart or a shattered human will, is one of the great keys of learning how to adjust in new territories—and to survive, thrive in, and reap the benefits of such transitions. It helps us trust that we will survive, and come up with means and creative ideas for taking advantage of new environments and the opportunities they bring. The ambitious spirit has a way of just being able to turn the sail in the direction that best fits the storm.

A taste of destiny

There is no good feeling like knowing who you were born to be and what you are destined to become. The feeling is extraordinary! It is a euphoric moment that cannot be bought with money or anything else. So how does ambition take part in this? My friends, the answer is clearer than it seems. Ambition is the secret agent within us that keeps us alive and moving long enough to get in touch with our destiny and purpose in life. Ambition is what keeps us persevering until we finally arrive at a place where we can taste our own God-given destiny. Without it, that first taste would always elude us.

The right normal

In this day and age, people tend to scorn the idea of being ambitious. They try to make it look abnormal and negative to be ambitious. This foolish ideology never comes from people who desire to achieve great things; rather, it comes from people who are stuck in their way of think-ing, people who are bound by an old system or traditions that do not work and are not productive, people who are stagnant and telling everyone else it's OK to be so, as well. These people are everywhere and in every avenue of life. Some even know how to put on a suit and a tie, but they are as stuck and un-productive as a swamp that never moves. And, just like a dead swamp, they bring out a smell and pollution that contaminate their surroundings and make it very hard to breathe the air of life. Their norm is mediocrity. Which is the wrong normal. But the norm of an ambitious person is to always keep moving, always keep exercising ideas and ful-filling goals. There is non-stop activity with such people, and it is just a matter of time before they begin to see the results they work so hard for, making it their "right normal."

Discovering identity

No one can discover their identity without really having the drive to do so. Ambition is one of the greatest tools in helping you reach a place of self-discovery. It is inevitable that, when we persevere with all we have, we will eventually reach our expected end, and ambition is one of the strengths that can carry us there. After we've discovered our identity and what we were born to be in life, ambition is a very strong advocate for helping us discover what that identity is *for*, and why it was given to us. Best of all, it helps us to search for places, circumstances, and surroundings in which our newfound identity and personal gifts can be most effective.

The champion within

There is no need to remind a champion-spirited person about ambi-tion, for they live it every day. It is so embedded within them that it has become a part of their everyday lives. Champions, as we know, always see amazing results as they press on toward their goals with positivity and perseverance, always seeking to improving every aspect of themselves and their lives. If the definition of ambition is having a strong desire to do and achieve something with all determination and hard work, then it is clearly safe to say that ambition is one of the main attributes of champions, pushing and fueling them to become the amazing people they see themselves becoming.

Experience is teacher

The journey or the preparation stages of an individual is not a very easy road. Sometimes, the weight can be very heavy and the challenges can be heartbreaking, but we persevere because we are determined that, whatever happened before or is currently happening, will get better—so much so that the painful experiences of the past will seem like nothing more than a shadow, having no effect on you. But the strength and wisdom you've attained because of those experiences will be an anchor that no one can remove.

The ambition to become something and the will to persevere no matter what has happened or is happening, helps us to endure long enough for our dreams and goals to come to fruition. An ambitious individual is ready to fight through any experiences, knowing they are lessons from which they can benefit, and believing that they're getting closer to their expected end.

Colliding with purpose

As we collide with purpose, we understand that ambition goes hand in hand with it. One will never be able to discover their God-given purpose if they don't have the drive to know it. Ambition is one of the main tools to help you keep going as the fire of life blazes within you and all around you, to the point where everything you know begins to burn away, in order to pave the way for a new state of mind and a new form of character, as you come to a place of self-discovery and purpose.

As we conclude, I hope I have helped you to understand that ambition is not the evil attribute that mediocre minds have claimed it to be. It is a very good asset to have and express if it falls into the hands of one who possesses the character, integrity, and will to become all that they can be, in order to change their own lives, the lives of those around them, and even those living on the other side of the world.

I'll say it again: Ambition is not the problem. It is a gift, and one that can only be brought forth or exercised according to the character of the individual carrying it.

What is your character?

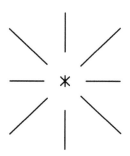